Charles Eustis Hubbard

The Campaign of the Forty-Fifth Regiment

Massachusetts Volunteer Militia

Charles Eustis Hubbard

The Campaign of the Forty-Fifth Regiment
Massachusetts Volunteer Militia

ISBN/EAN: 9783337268770

Printed in Europe, USA, Canada, Australia, Japan

Cover: Foto ©ninafisch / pixelio.de

More available books at **www.hansebooks.com**

THE CADET REGIMENT.

BOSTON:
PRINTED BY JAMES S. ADAMS
1882.

Published by the "Company A Associates" of the Forty-Fifth Regiment, M. V. M.

PREFACE.

NOT long after the return of the Forty-Fifth Massachusetts regiment from North Carolina, an informal meeting of some of the members of Company A was held in Boston, which resulted in the formation of a permanent association, known as the "Co. A Associates of the 45th Regt. Mass. Vol. Mil."

This association has proved a constant source of pleasure to its members, and has served to keep in fresh remembrance the many and varied experiences of our campaign. The annual reunions are held on the anniversary of the expedition to Trenton, and from year to year the friendships which were formed in the service so many years ago, are renewed. The presence of some of the officers as invited guests often adds to the pleasure of the occasion.

Not a little of the success of these yearly meetings is due to that warm friend of the company and regiment, Colonel Edward W. Kinsley. As, in the old war time, no guest was ever more welcome than he, whether in camp at Readville, on the deck of the "Mississippi," in the city of Newbern, or on the sand-plains of North Carolina, so it has been in the time of peace at our reunions. Elected an honorary member of the "Co. A Associates," the meetings would be incomplete, indeed, without his cheery presence to enliven us with reminiscence or song, or, better still, to give us a bit of the inner history of the dark days in '62 and '63, with which he is so familiar, and in which he played so important a part.

The question of publishing a history of the campaign of the 45th has been often discussed at these Company A meetings, and a committee was even appointed to consider the matter. The subject has also been under consideration in the Regimental Association, organized some years since. But nothing was done by either association, until at the meeting of the Co. A Associates, held in January last, it was definitely voted to publish a history of our campaign, with illustrations, and a committee was chosen for this purpose. This book is the result, and in offering it to the members and friends of the regiment, the committee desire to make this explanation.

Shortly after the regiment was mustered out of the service, one of the members of Company A wrote a brief history of the campaign, not with any view to publication, but for his own private gratification, and to preserve the leading incidents of his army experiences. He induced another member of the company, now a well-known Boston artist, to illustrate the manuscript with drawings copied from sketches taken during our army life.

This history has been read with interest by different members of the regiment, and the committee were convinced that it would be far better to obtain, as they have done, permission of the writer and artist to publish, without alteration, this illustrated story of the campaign, written when the scenes described were fresh in the mind, than to attempt the publication of an elaborate history of the regiment, even if it were possible to induce any member to undertake such a task at this late date.

In justice to our comrades who have kindly granted us this privilege, the committee feel sure, if any apology is needed, that the reader will bear in mind the fact that this joint effort is the production of their youth, and not the work of to-day.

BOSTON, June, 1882.

CONTENTS.

CHAPTER.
- I. CAMP LIFE AT READVILLE.
- II. THE VOYAGE.
- III. CAMP AMORY ON THE TRENT.
- IV. ON THE MARCH.
- V. OUR BATTLES.
- VI. THE RETURN.
- VII. A TRIP TO TRENTON.
- VIII. LIFE IN NEWBERN.
- IX. THE GRAND REVIEW.
- X. THE FOURTEENTH OF MARCH.
- XI. A TRIP UP THE RAILROAD.
- XII. CAMP MASSACHUSETTS.
- XIII. HOMEWARD BOUND.

ILLUSTRATIONS.

	PAGE
CAMP MEIGS AT READVILLE, (*Frontispiece*).	
OUTWARD BOUND, FORT MACON, ETC.,	11
CAMP AMORY ON THE TRENT,	21
BATTLE OF KINSTON,	31
KINSTON SWAMP AND PLAN OF BATTLE-GROUND,	39
BATTLE OF GOLDSBORO,	49
RESERVE PICKET-STATION, BLOCKHOUSE, ETC.,	57
QUARTERS OF CO. A., NEWBERN, (Front View,)	67
QUARTERS OF CO. A., NEWBERN, (Rear View,)	77
FIELD AND STAFF, 45th M. V. M.,	87
UP THE RAILROAD, DOVER CROSS-ROADS, ETC.,	97
NEWBERN, CAMP MASSACHUSETTS, ETC.,	107
COMPANY A AT READVILLE,	117

ROSTER

OF

FORTY-FIFTH REGIMENT, M. V. M.

CHARLES R. CODMAN,	*Colonel.*
OLIVER W. PEABODY,	*Lieutenant Colonel.*
RUSSELL STURGIS, JR.,	*Major.*
SAMUEL KNEELAND,	*Surgeon.*
JOSHUA B. TREADWELL,	*Assistant Surgeon.*
DANIEL McLEAN,	*Assistant Surgeon.*
GERSHOM C. WINSOR,	*Adjutant.*
FRANCIS A. DEWSON,	*Quartermaster.*
ANDREW L. STONE,	*Chaplain.*
HENRY G. WHEELOCK,	*Sergeant Major.*
ARTHUR REED,	*Quartermaster Sergeant.*
CHARLES F. RICHARDSON,	*Commissary Sergeant.*
EDWARD WIGGLESWORTH, JR.,	*Hospital Steward.*
THEODORE PARKMAN,	*Color Sergeant.*

COMPANY A.

GEORGE P. DENNY,	*Captain.*
GEORGE E. POND,	*1st Lieutenant.*
EDWARD B. RICHARDSON,	*2d Lieutenant.*

COMPANY B.

JOSEPH M. CHURCHILL,	*Captain.*
WILLIAM S. BOND,	*1st Lieutenant.*
ABIJAH HOLLIS,	*2d Lieutenant.*

COMPANY C.

EDWARD J. MINOT,	Captain.
HARRISON GARDNER,	1st Lieutenant.
LEWIS R. WHITTAKER,	2d Lieutenant.

COMPANY D.

NAT'L WILLIS BUMSTEAD,	Captain.
SAMUEL THAXTER,	1st Lieutenant.
CYRUS A. SEARS,	2d Lieutenant.

COMPANY E.

THOMAS B. WALES, JR.,	Captain.
ALPHEUS H. HARDY,	1st Lieutenant.
J. FRANK EMMONS,	2d Lieutenant.

COMPANY F.

EDWARD F. DALAND,	Captain.
SAMUEL C. ELLIS,	1st Lieutenant.
THEODORE C. HURD,	2d Lieutenant.

COMPANY G.

JOSEPH MURDOCH,	Captain.
THEODORE A. THAYER,	1st Lieutenant.
BENJAMIN H. TICKNOR,	2d Lieutenant, promoted.
M. EVERETT WARE,	2d Lieutenant.

COMPANY H.

LEWIS W. TAPPAN, JR.,	Captain.
ALFRED WINSOR, JR.,	1st Lieutenant.
ALFRED K. POST,	2d Lieutenant.

COMPANY I.

CHARLES O. RICH,	Captain.
J. DIXWELL THOMPSON,	1st Lieutenant.
EDWARD R. BLAGDEN,	2d Lieutenant.

COMPANY K.

GEORGE H. HOMANS,	Captain.
CHARLES A. WALKER,	1st Lieutenant.
JOHN H. ROBINSON,	2d Lieutenant.

ROLL OF COMPANY A.

FORTY-FIFTH REGIMENT, M. V. M.

GEORGE P. DENNY, Captain.

GEORGE E. POND, 1st Lieutenant.   EDW. H. RICHARDSON, 2d Lieut.

CHARLES W. BARSTOW, Ord. Sergt.   WM. E. WHEATON, 4th Sergeant.
GEORGE H. WATSON, 2d Sergeant.   GEO. F. WOODMAN, 5th Sergeant.
WILLIAM R. BUTLER, 3d Sergeant.   (Promoted.)
   (Died Jan. 26, 1867.)   CHARLES B. SUMNER, 5th Sergeant.

LUTHER F. ALLEN, 1st Corporal.   ALBERT A. CHITTENDEN, 6th Corp'l.
AUGUSTUS S. LOVETT, 2d Corporal.   WILLIAM F. SHAW, 7th Corporal.
CHAS. EUSTIS HUBBARD, 3d Corporal.   (Died Nov. 15, 1871.)
ERROL GRANT, 4th Corporal.   WILLIAM B. STACY, 7th Corporal.
HENRY K. PORTER, 5th Corporal.   HENRY E. MERRIAM, 8th Corporal.

SAMUEL L. ALLEN.   EDMUND W. BUSS.
NATHANIEL ANDREWS.   MOSES J. COLMAN.
WM. B. ATKINSON.   EDMUND P. DAVENPORT.
CALEB L. BATES.   (Died 1878.)
   (Died Oct. 15, 1864.)   FRANKLIN H. DEAN.
CYRUS H. BATES.   REUBEN EDGETT.
WILLIAM H. BECKET.   JOHN B. EDMANDS.
CHARLES H. BENNETT.   GEO. W. ESTABROOK.
WILLIAM H. BERRY.   FRANK A. FIELD.
JOSEPH H. BINGHAM.   CALVIN W. FITCH.
HENRY S. BLISS.   JOHN W. FOWLE.
CHARLES H. BROOKS.   (Died July 8, 1863.)
GEORGE BROOKS.   GEO. E. FOX.
   (Died Feb. 10, 1863.)   (Died Jan. 10, 1863.)
ELIAS W. BOURNE.   JOSEPH V. FREELAND.
LOUIS H. BOUTELLE.   (Died May 10, 1872.)

ROLL OF COMPANY A.

Rufus P. Furguson.
Stephen A. Furguson.
   (Died July 17, 1863.)
Gardner Gilman.
Chas. P. Goldsmith.
Elbridge Graves.
   (Died Dec. 17, 1862.)
Chas. H. Griffin.
Chas. A. Gross.
Abraham G. R. Hale.
E. Thomas Hale.
   (Died Sept. 7, 1868.)
Milo T. Hardy.
Francis P. Haskell.
Robert Hasty.
Horace Holmes.
   (Died Aug. 19, 1864.)
Chas. A. Howard.
Rodolphus K. Howard.
Levi D. Jones.
Thomas Kinsley.
Silas W. Lang.
Charles H. Leonard.
Richard H. Lincoln.
Stephen Lincoln.
   (Died June 30, 1863.)
Jeremiah R. Lord.
Edmund S. Lunt.
Albert W. Mann.
James H. Mason.
Joseph A. Morgan.
   (Died July 3, 1863.)
Edwin T. Morse.
John R. Morse.
Henry D. Norton.
Geo. B. Parker.
   (Died ———.)

Daniel Pert.
Francis B. Pert.
Wm. J. Pert.
Wm. P. Plimpton.
Wm. Poland.
Wm. H. Pratt.
Frank L. Putnam.
Wm. A. Richards.
Swartz Richardson.
   (Died Dec. 1, 1872.)
Oscar W. Sargent.
   (Died Oct. 19, 1877.)
Henry B. Scudder.
Frank H. Shapleigh.
Samuel B. Shapleigh.
Thomas W. Shapleigh.
Rufus S. Smith.
   (Died ———.)
Jeffrey T. Stanley.
Henry R. Thompson.
Edwin E. Tiffany.
Geo. W. Tower.
   (Died Jan. 20, 1871.)
Chas. A. Vinal.
John H. Watson.
   (Died Oct. 22, 1873.)
Isaac G. Wheeler.
L. Henry Whitney.
Israel D. Wildes.
Lyman D. Willcut.
Geo. Willmonton.
Henry T. Winslow.
   (Died June 30, 1863.)

Honorary Member.
Edw. W. Kinsley.

THE FORTY-FIFTH.

CHAPTER I.

CAMP-LIFE AT READVILLE.

SHORTLY after the President's call for three hundred thousand nine months' men, in the summer of 1862, a meeting was held by the Independent Corps of Cadets, in their armory in Boston, to consider the expediency of organizing a nine months' regiment, of which that corps should be, as it were, the nucleus. The proposition being favorably received, application was speedily made to Governor Andrew by various members in favor of the movement, for permission to recruit for such a regiment, under the title of the Cadet Regiment, but officially to be known as the Forty-fifth Regiment Massachusetts Volunteer Militia.

Charles R. Codman of Boston, then adjutant of the cadets, was selected as future commander of the regiment, subject, however, to the approval of the line officers, who were themselves to be elected by their respective companies in accordance with the militia law of the state, prior to receiving their commissions from the governor. Recruiting officers canvassed the state, and the companies ranked in the order in which their respective rolls were filled.

Readville was selected as the rendezvous and camping-ground for the regiment, and on the twelfth of September, Company D went into camp at that place, followed at intervals by the other companies as they severally attained a size which would warrant a respectable appearance on drill and parade.

The camp was pleasantly situated on high ground, surrounded on three sides by other camps, while the fourth was skirted by woods, back of which, as a fitting background, rose the blue hills of Milton in all their beauty.

We were quartered in barracks, long wooden sheds running parallel to each other, and perpendicular to and facing the parade-ground. Back of each barrack, and separated by a street some twenty feet in width, were the little cook-houses, while still farther to the rear were the officers' quarters, quartermaster's department, etc.

The first night in camp was a novel one to most of us, and formed the entrance to a new phase of existence, a military life. We marched from the depot and were received with shouts of welcome by the companies already in camp. Halting in front of the barrack assigned us, the order to break ranks was the signal for a simultaneous rush of all to take possession of the movable bunks, which in two tiers lined both sides of the building, followed by another stampede after straw to fill them.

My first military duty was the scouring of sundry rusty pots and pans preparatory to the evening meal. All the true patriots came into camp with empty haversacks, determined to brave the soldier's fare at the outset, and our pride was at its height when, formed in line, we marched single file to the cook-house, and had doled out to us from its window, the huge slice of bread and dipper of coffee or tea.

"Truly, we are serving our country at last," we said, and ate our rations without thought of what we had left behind; but that slice of bread, varied often by hard-tack, so often, indeed, that the bread was the exception, and the dipper of coffee soon became an old, very old story, and the good things at home would rise in our memories, the ghosts of better times, and would not down at our bidding, nor would the hard-tack, either.

The interval between supper and roll-call was wisely spent in making our bunks comfortable for the night; and that first night the custom was instituted by our captain, of reading the lesson and prayers for the day after morning and evening roll-call; and was faithfully continued until the regiment went into tents, some seven months later.

Punctually at nine, taps sounded and the lights were extinguished, and as reveille was at half-past five, we naturally desired and expected to lose ourselves immediately; but alas! for the fallacy of human hopes, not an eye in that barrack was closed in sleep a moment before midnight, except, perhaps, that of one of our number, afterwards discharged for deafness. The evil one himself was, without doubt, on a rampage that night, and raised a very bedlam in our midst.

In vain did the orderly threaten; in vain did the officer of the day, encircled by that mysterious sash at which we raw ones had gazed with awe, command silence. For a moment there would be a lull in the storm, deluding the sober-minded into a belief that quiet was at length restored, when, with a laugh or a jest, the uproar would burst forth with redoubled vigor. Even after sheer exhaustion had quieted the unruly ones, it was hard to sleep as we lay thinking over our strange situation, and at intervals through the night caught the distant challenge of the sentry at the approach of the welcome relief. But the longest day must have an end, and at last our weary eyelids were closed not to open again till the loud beat of the drum summoned us from the land of dreams.

With the return of the day our new duties commenced; some were detailed for camp guard, others for police duty, but most of us were marched out to drill, and during our nine months' service this proved an unfailing source of amusement and occupation, and was improved to the utmost by the officers.

Police duty has a mysterious sound to the uninitiated, and those first detailed for that service had their expectations raised to a great height, but the fall was so much the more severe. Some were set to work digging wells, others to sweep up the camp with brooms of their own manufacture, and one squad were assigned the task of emptying the barrels in the rear of the cook-houses, filled with the refuse of the men's rations; police duty is, in fact, to enact the part of general scavenger for the camp, a very necessary, but at the same time disagreeable, business.

Our first day's guard duty was an experience never to be forgotten. The solitary march back and forth back and forth, in the same narrow path, rain or shine, warm or cold, can only be appreciated after actual trial. Never did time fly with such tardy wings as in the night-watches of those dark, wet, fall nights, when the approach of the relief was to the weary sentinel like a release from imprisonment. But those first experiences had their comical side as well. The awkward manner of handling the guns, the stupidity displayed in learning the instructions and duties of the post, and the various mistakes constantly occurring were laughable to witness.

One day there was a more than usually difficult subject, whose mistakes furnished a fund of amusement for the whole guard. After innumerable blunders during the day, at nightfall he was carefully and at great length instructed with regard to the countersign, its object, nature, etc., until the lieutenant of the guard thought he would be able to pass muster under the ordeal of the grand round, but the officer, by skillful questioning, discovered that the countersign was in his belief a sort of counterfeit bill, which was to be passed on delivery, — to say the least, an original interpretation of the meaning of the word.

But the mistakes and blunders were by no means confined to the men, for the officers could, without breach of modesty, lay claim to their full share. One was particularly noted for his ignorance of military knowledge, and had earned, among the men, the soubriquet of "Right Backward Dress," from his repeated blunders in reference to that order; while another, having occasion to salute the commandant of the post, managed to bring his guard to the "present," but then gave the order "stack arms," quite regardless of the intermediate orders essential to a proper execution of the manœuvre.

On pleasant days, guard duty at the camp entrance was by no means disagreeable, for on such days the stream of visitors was unceasing from morning till night. How we all enjoyed those visits! and the sight of a friend in the distance was a never-failing pretext for an excuse from drill or parade. We were always ready to relieve them of the baskets and bundles they labored under, and of course they must inspect the barracks, admire the various decorations and inscriptions that ornamented the different bunks, and wonder how any mortal could ever sleep in such boxes.

One afternoon, two of us were made happy by the arrival of a carriage-load of friends, who had come to dress-parade. We both noticed several mysterious-looking baskets stowed away in the depths of the carriage, but of course no remark was made as to their probable contents. After witnessing and duly admiring the parade, at the sound of the supper-call, the ladies invited us to take supper with them, if we could for once deny ourselves the pleasures of the government commissariat. So, nothing loath, we were armed with the above-mentioned baskets, and took up our line of march toward a grassy knoll, back of the camp and outside the lines, to avoid intrusion, and there, stretched out on shawls and blankets, we had a supper worthy of the name.

As we lay about the grass, taking our meal, the full moon rose in all its beauty from behind the Milton hills, and lit up the quiet October evening till the camps and hills were flooded with the silvery light. The growing dampness warned us at last to shorten our pleasure, but on taking refuge in the barrack, we were agreeably surprised by an impromptu concert from visitors and hosts, and as our regiment boasted some very good voices, the singing formed an appropriate ending to such a delightful evening. We enjoyed one or two moonlight evenings in rather a different way, marching about the camp, headed by the band, and blundering through some of the simpler battalion movements for the colonel's benefit.

Our battalion drills in those days were very amusing, for though in company drill the men got the blame for all mistakes, yet here the burden of reproof was shifted to the officers' shoulders, and this was in some measure a recompense to us, for the laugh was now on our side. The tortures undergone by the colonel, in those early days, in witnessing the officers' oft-repeated blunders, must have been truly excruciating. Now one, then another, would fall the victim of his censuring tongue, until, bewildered by the flying sarcasms and the complication of manœuvres, their confusion became worse confounded, and we of the file, rejoicing over the misfortunes of the rank, would hail with delight the welcome command of "Drill is dismissed," screamed forth by the colonel, half an hour before the usual time.

Nor did we depend on visitors or drill for our whole stock of amusement. Bathing formed a part of the daily routine while the weather permitted, and foot-ball was a favorite occupation during our leisure hours. Our evenings passed quickly in a quiet rubber of whist, or in listening to the music with which the singers often favored us, usually in the barrack, but occasionally on the mild fall evenings, in the open air, stretched lazily on the grass before the door.

But the crowning feature of our life at Camp Meigs was the dress-parade, and this would be an incomplete history indeed, had that been omitted in the tale. Very modest in appearance at the outset, with thin ranks, but two or three drummers and those far from perfect, and more than all, no guns for the men; they were gradually improved, now by fresh recruits, then by the addition of the band, and the arrival of our Springfield rifles, until, under this combination of improvements, we were enabled to present a very respectable appearance.

It seems like a dream to recall the two long rows of people which night after night stood facing each other in front of the barracks,—the actors and spectators. We come to parade-rest, and the performance commences. Three groans from the band, then the inevitable — the show tune of the band; and as they come slowly marching down the line, we see a familiar but ever novel sight. A little in advance of the band, monarch of all he surveys, and the "cynosure of neighboring eyes," struts Mariani, the drum-major, pride of the regiment, twirling his baton, token of empire, giving that finish to the show which even our rival neighbors are prone to admire. Never afterwards did the band play that familiar old tune, No. 45, on the sand-plains of North Carolina, but a smile ran down the line; and as our thoughts reverted to the pleasant dress-parades at Readville, we longed for that opposite row of faces, that we might show our friends what a good parade was like.

The twenty-sixth of September, eight companies were mustered into the service of the United States; and on the eighth of October, the remaining companies,—together with the field and staff officers,— and we became an organized regiment under the

United States, though constituting a part of the state militia.

It had been supposed all along that the Army of the Potomac would be our destination, but when the 44th sailed for Newbern, it became a settled fact that North Carolina was to be our arena also, and as the day of departure drew near, every hour of our short furloughs became precious and the visits of our friends even more frequent and pleasant than before.

The last Sunday but one, about half the regiment marched to Milton, and there took the cars for Boston, where we attended service at Park Street Church, the church of our chaplain, Rev. A. L. Stone, D. D. After an appropriate farewell discourse, we returned to camp much pleased with our trip, with a good appetite for the regular Sunday dinner in camp of baked beans.

On Saturday, the first of November, the colors were presented to the regiment by Governor Andrew, and were received by Colonel Codman in our behalf. It was a gala day in camp, and the grounds were covered with visitors, many present for the last time, as the regiment was under marching orders. In the evening an impromptu mock dress-parade was quite successfully carried out, much to the amusement of the spectators, who still lingered, reluctant to say good-bye.

The last day or two was full of bustle and confusion and all who could obtain furloughs were at home, leave-taking and making their final arrangements. Wednesday, the fifth of November, dawned on us at last, raw and disagreeable, and with full knapsacks and full hearts as well, we bade farewell to old Camp Meigs, where we had passed a month and a half so pleasantly. Perhaps at the time we did not realize fully all our advantages at Readville, being new to the life, but we have certainly appreciated them in the retrospect, and those of our number who may take the field again will reap the full benefit of their early experience.

Leaving the cars at the Boston depot, we formed our line, and escorted by our patrons and godfathers, the Cadets, marched directly to the Common, where, on the Beacon mall, a collation was spread to which ample justice was done.

After receiving our remaining colors from the hands of the governor (the regiment carried three flags, United States, State and Regimental), and hearing addresses, very appropriate, no doubt, but so long that we were ready to drop with fatigue, loaded down as we were with full equipments, the last good-byes were said, and we started en route for the wharf.

It was, indeed, a proud moment of our lives, the march that day through the crowded streets of old Boston, elate with the consciousness that we were embarked in a righteous cause, and determined to play our parts like men.

THE HALT

CHAPTER II.

THE VOYAGE.

THE mere recollection of the nine days passed on the steamer "Mississippi" is painful, but it occupied too prominent a position in our experience to be omitted in this sketch.

After the usual delay on the wharf, attending the embarkation of a large body of men, we filed on to the steamer, and were ushered into our respective quarters. Our company, with five others, were consigned to the stern of the vessel; so, passing down the companion-way, deeper and deeper, darker and darker, until we could, at least, claim a nearer proximity to China than ever before, we arrived in the hold. As light was never known to penetrate that quarter, for two dim lanterns and three air-holes covered with gratings could hardly be said to afford light, it will be impossible to describe its appearance. As well as could be ascertained by touch and smell, the whole available space was fitted up with bunks, three tiers deep and of different capacities, holding from one to four occupants, those comfortably crowded with three being intended for four, and so on down to the single ones. All this we learned by the touch, and at least we will give them credit for making the most of their room; but our olfactory nerves had another story to tell; however, we will not particularize.

The other companies were stowed in the forward part of the vessel, between decks and in the hold, the band lying wherever they could find space enough. In addition, five companies of the 46th Regiment were entrusted to the tender mercies of the "Mississippi," and where they were packed is beyond the power of man to say — one company, at all events, was located on the quarter-deck.

Now all this would have been well enough had we sailed that night, as was intended, and made the four-day trip to Beaufort; but no such good luck was in store, and our initiation was not to be quite so easy. A heavy northeasterly storm set in, soon after we had hauled into the stream, and for five days, a tempest of rain, hail, sleet and snow raged with unceasing fury.

Colonel Codman declared the vessel should not sail in such a crowded, filthy condition, and the captain said he could not sail if he would, on account of the storm, and more than that, there must be a convoy to protect us from the "Alabama," at that time reported off the coast. So there we lay at anchor, tossing and pitching, in plain sight of the city, which only served to aggravate us in our wretchedness, while near by, lay our companions in misery, the 43d and the remainder of the 46th on our consort, the "Merrimac."

Our drinking-water was condensed from salt water by an apparatus connected with the engine, and was always in a lukewarm, yellowish state, enough to make one renounce water forever, and before which Gough himself would have stood dumb. A guard, also, was always stationed over the cask to prevent the men from drinking too much; whether because the process of condensation had rendered it more precious than common water, or from a fear of the men sickening from a too free use of the vile liquid, is still an unexplained mystery. May the inventor be condemned to have it for an eternal drink!

The food given us baffles all attempt at description. The filthy messes of soup, salt-junk and burnt rice were boiled in the same huge caldron, and the sight of the dirty cook added to one taste of the unknown compound, called by some familiar name calculated to deceive us, was enough to make one eager to die of starvation. It was so pleasant, just before dinner, to be ordered below to await our turn in the long line, and on the way down, catch a glimpse of the cabin table, covered with delicacies fresh from the Boston markets, and when our company was called, to ascend from the depths of the vessel, cup in hand, eager for the sumptuous repast doled out from the great boiler, which, like the magician's flask, furnished tea, coffee, soup, etc., as desired. Yet all this was on a first-class transport;—may heaven take pity on the poor wretches whose hard fate consigns them to vessels of an inferior class!

After strenuous exertions by our colonel and some good friends of the regiment in the city, another steamer, the "Saxon," was provided for the 46th, and our own vessel underwent a partial cleansing. We were also visited by some of the more enterprising of our friends, who ventured down the harbor in a tug during the lulls of the storm, and having received an invoice of lanterns, books and eatables, we were enabled to make ourselves rather more comfortable.

We embarked on Wednesday, and on the following Monday, accompanied by the "Merrimac," "Saxon," and the gun-boat "Huron," we steamed down the harbor just at sunset, overjoyed at the prospect of a quick voyage and a speedy release from our uncomfortable quarters. Two or three of us had, in the course of our wanderings, discovered a cosy little nook in the extreme stern of the vessel, in close proximity to the screw, and here, away from the forlorn, grumbling crowd, which thronged the decks and holds, with our lanterns, books and cards, we managed to while away the weary hours quite pleasantly.

The storm had completely exhausted itself, and the weather was all that could be desired; and though the slowness of our consort, the "Huron," delayed us somewhat, yet after we were once fairly started on our way, nothing occurred to mar the voyage, and on Friday morning, the 14th instant, the lights of Beaufort harbor were visible, and our trials on shipboard were at an end. Our decks were crowded with a happy company, and an exciting race ensued between the "Mississippi" and the "Merrimac," for the pilot-boat which lay off the entrance of the harbor, awaiting our approach; but, to the chagrin of our captain, and in fact of us all, the "Merrimac" came out ahead, and having been boarded by the pilot, proceeded slowly in advance, the "Mississippi" following closely in her wake, without delaying for a second pilot.

It was a perfect morning, and the soft, fresh breeze was very different from the cold wintery blasts we had left behind us in Boston harbor. Every object visible was scanned with curious eyes as we entered the bay and began to thread the channel, rendered very intricate by the low sand-bars which lay in every direction. These were covered with sea-fowl of every description, while the myriads of ducks which blackened the water, made us wish for gun and dog with unceasing and unsatisfied longing.

Two or three gun-boats were riding at anchor in the harbor, and their sides were lined with a row of bronzed faces, whose owners cheered us heartily as we passed slowly by. Fort Macon, of Burnside fame, soon made its appearance on our left, its guns commanding both land and water in all directions, and its ramparts dotted with the garrison who welcomed us as we drew near. The fort is apparently on an island, but is really on the point of a long neck of land running back for some miles before uniting with the main. It has been greatly strengthened since it came into our hands, and, in conjunction with the gun-boats, bids defiance to any foe.

Beaufort lies on the opposite side of the harbor, and presents a very pretty appearance as seen at a distance from the water, but does not improve on a closer acquaintance. The attention is immediately attracted by a large white building standing on the very edge of the water, resting under the shadow of the Stars and Stripes. Formerly the hotel of the place and the summer resort of North Carolinians, it no longer echoes to the tread of the *élite* of Newbern, but as a government hospital is filled with the poor fellows parched with the fevers which all summer infest the sand-plains on the Neuse, and who doubtless enjoy the cool breezes from the Atlantic.

and the delicious sea-bath quite as much as those who formerly thronged the place.

Soon the depot came in sight, and there stood the long train of platform cars, waiting to convey some of us to our destination. The idea of spending another night on the water was almost unendurable, but suddenly we perceived quite a commotion on the decks of our leader, and to our great delight it was soon evident that she was aground. Feeling our way, as it were, step by step, we drew nearer, and a perfect yell of exultation went up from our vessel as we glided by our discomfited rival, and, rejoicing over our victory, steamed alongside the wharf of what was once the Atlantic and North Carolina Railroad, but now is known as the United States Military Railroad.

We were quickly disembarked, and soon closely packed on the open freight cars, rather a novel mode of conveyance to most of us, but one to be recommended as admirably adapted to sight-seeing, and in pleasant weather both airy and agreeable. Leaving the 43d and 46th to pass another night on shipboard, our train was soon on its way to Newbern, distant about forty miles. Our first stop was at Morehead City, though why called "city" it would be hard to say, as it contains but a few miserable houses and a forlorn-looking hotel, famous as the residence, for a time, of Company C of the 45th, who were quartered there as garrison. Every little while a picket-station would come in view, and now and then a camp whose occupants greeted us with shouts of welcome and inquiries as to our State, number of our regiment, latest news, etc. A blockhouse commanding the bridge over a small creek was a novelty, and, as long as daylight lasted, we found enough that was new and interesting to keep our eyes fully occupied. The country itself through which the road passes is wholly devoid of interest—in fact, a vast swamp covered with pine forests, which extend over a great part of the eastern section of the state; tar, pitch and turpentine being correctly given by the geography as among the principal productions.

It was quite dark when the train drew near the town of Newbern, and slowly crossing the long bridge which spans the river Trent, passed up what we afterwards discovered to be Hancock street, lighted, to our great astonishment, with gas. We finally came to a halt before a long freight-house, where a quantity of oats was stored in bags. This building was assigned to the right wing as their quarters for the night, and after our cramped bunks on shipboard, we found the oat-bags very acceptable. The left wing passed the night in some vacant tents near at hand.

As we were decidedly cold and hungry after our ride, the arrival of some of the 44th Mass., with pails of hot coffee, was very opportune, and we regaled them with the latest news from home in return for their kindness. Their description of the hardships endured on the Tarboro' expedition, from which they had just returned, did not tend to heighten our already very far from pleasant impressions of North Carolina as a place of abode.

As we were taught the productions of North Carolina in our youth, the negro stood first on the list, and certainly we had seen no reason to belie that statement. We had not ceased laughing from the time we landed, at the comical figures which met us on every hand. It was the first object to meet our eye at the wharf, and I doubt not the last thing visible as we left the shores of Beaufort on our return. We no longer wondered where the minstrels at the north procured their absurd costumes; here was material for an endless variety. It was better than any play simply to walk about and examine the different styles of dress, for this was before anything had been done at the north for the contrabands, and they appeared in the rags they had brought from their plantations. It was amusing to listen to the questions which greeted them from all sides, the bright answers often displaying more sense than did the questions. Some of our men seemed to have taken it for granted that all the tales they had read of the horrors of slavery were the general rule, and that the great aim and object of every master's life was to abuse and maltreat the slave in every possible way. The erroneous and absurd notions at first entertained by them of the state of southern society, could only be equalled by the opinions of our southern friends about the north. One question asked will serve as an illustration. We were grouped around a fire that first night, talking with some bright little contrabands, when one of our number asked one "If his master ever let him stand by such a nice fire as that," which in that land of pines certainly was rather ridiculous, and, for a Boston boy, rather an insult to his bringing up.

We employed the two or three hours of leisure the next morning in a tour of inspection through the town. With our eyes still dazzled with the bright effulgence of the New England metropolis, and unaccustomed to the darkness of that benighted land, we unhesitatingly pronounced it the meanest, dirtiest spot we had ever set foot in. But it did not take many weeks of camp life, where the only houses visible were the barracks and a few miserable negro hovels, to create a very decided change in our views upon this subject, as well as on many others of like nature.

The town is very prettily situated at the confluence of the Neuse and Trent, the former between one and two miles wide at this point, the latter something less than a mile. It is laid out quite regularly and abounds in elms and flower gardens, many of them very beautiful, and relieving the otherwise ugly streets. We became better, in fact most intimately, acquainted with the place when we were quartered there, and a more minute description will be found further on. Our first impressions received that morning were, however, certainly the reverse of pleasant.

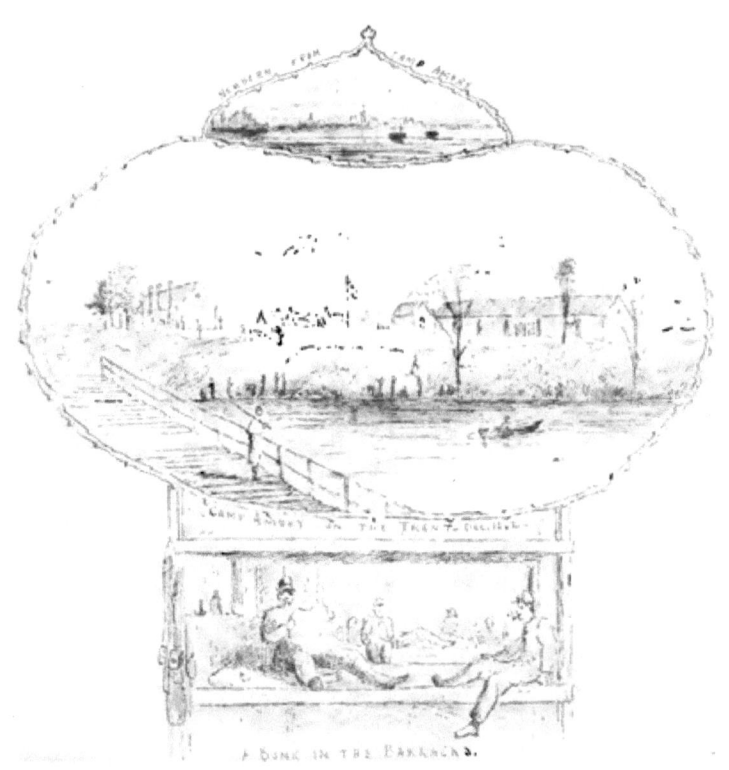

CHAPTER III.

CAMP AMORY ON THE TRENT.

RETURNING to the freight house where the night had been spent, we shouldered our guns and knapsacks and started en route for our new home. Passing through the town, and recrossing the railroad bridge, we left the line of the railroad and took the road running along the edge of the Trent. After toiling through the sand for about a mile, we came upon a negro settlement and a long row of stables, once rebel cavalry quarters, now used for government team horses and as a sort of wagon station. An old canal boat, mounting two heavy guns, commands the spot as well as the surrounding country, which has been cleared of trees on both sides of the river to give free range to the artillery.

Shortly after leaving this dirty village, the barracks assigned us came in view, about half a mile up the river, a most welcome sight, for the day was hot, the road very sandy and our load heavy. The 17th Mass. were encamped in tents near by, and as our regiment approached, they turned out to meet us and give us welcome. Poor fellows! they looked forlorn enough, thin and pale, almost all of them having had the chills or some fever through the summer, from which they were just recovering, a great part of the regiment being still in hospital.

On reaching our destination, knapsacks were quickly unslung, and we hastened to inspect our new quarters. The barracks — unlike those at Readville — consisted of two long buildings, each arranged for five companies. They were at right angles with the river, and parallel to each other, some three hundred feet apart. The hospital tents were located midway between the buildings, but after a time the hospital was transferred to the barracks, rendered vacant by the detail of two of the companies. The officers occupied tents, which were pitched away from and opposite the river, facing and forming one side of a quadrangle, enclosed by the river, the barracks and the tents. Beyond the officers' quarters was the parade-ground, while the drill-ground lay in every direction.

Directly in the rear of the north barrack, ran the main road from Newbern south to Beaufort, crossing the Trent at this point, on what is called the County bridge. The bridge was commanded at that time by a little earthwork, called Fort Gaston, which mounted two guns, to all appearance more dangerous to those in their rear than in their front; this celebrated fort was for a long time garrisoned by one man detailed regularly from the camp guard.

An immense plain stretched out in front of us, some two or three miles in length, and a mile in width, bounded in our rear by the river, and skirted on all sides by fine forests. For the last two or three years, these have been gradually disappearing before the axe of the pioneer, thus leaving the approach to the city from this direction wholly under command of gun-boats on either of the rivers.

On the edge of the woods, on the opposite side of the plain, gleamed the white tents of the 23d Mass., just relieved from provost duty. The 43d went into camp a short distance beyond us, and not many weeks after our own arrival, the 51st Mass. were quartered in the barracks next beyond ours.

The camp took its name from Colonel Amory of the 17th Mass., who had command of our brigade, composed at first of the 17th, 23d, 43d, and 45th Mass. Later, the 51st Mass. took the place of the 23d, when the latter regiment was ordered into another department.

The first day or two was spent in establishing ourselves comfortably in our new quarters, writing letters, undergoing an inspection by our corps commander, Gen. Foster, and strolling about the adjacent country, seeing the sights and making friends with our neighbors, black as well as white. The camp swarmed with contrabands of all ages and both sexes, some with eatables to sell, apples, pies, cakes, biscuit and sweet potatoes, others wanting to take in washing. The boys wished to hire out as servants, and at such cheap rates that we all immediately had one attached to us, as a sort of body-guard, to run errands, draw water, wash dishes, and live on our leavings.

The negro huts in the vicinity of the camp were often visited by the curious, and the mode of life in them afforded us much pleasure, as it was at the same time novel and amusing. "Ole Aunt Gatsy" was quite a favorite with a select few who had discovered her various excellencies, and we were indebted to her cuisine for many a nice meal. Her method of cooking seemed very strange to eyes accustomed to ranges and stoves, and is worthy of mention. All the cooking is done at an open wood fire, the chimney always standing outside the house. The principal implement of cookery is an iron pot with short legs and a flat iron cover, somewhat larger than the mouth of the pot. After raking out a nice bed of coals, the food, no matter whether a bake, roast or boil, is placed in the pot over the coals, and the cover is kept constantly sprinkled with fresh coals until the contents are cooked. They also use the ordinary stew-pan, and earthen ovens in which they build huge fires, and, after the earth is thoroughly heated, put in the meat or whatever it may be, close both door and chimney, and in due time produce a joint of beef, or a dish of baked beans fit for the most epicurean New Englander.

We soon settled down into a quiet, monotonous life of drill and guard duty, more wearisome than arduous. The broad expanse of plain which stretched out before our camp was large enough for an army to manœuvre upon, and the officers certainly made the most of their opportunity, for company, battalion and brigade drills followed one another so closely that one had scarcely time to think in the intervening moments. A very semi-occasional visit to town served as a pleasant little episode, by giving us a glimpse of an approach at least to a civilized existence, thereby preventing us from wholly lapsing into barbarism.

Nor were our Sundays by any means days of rest; for as regularly as the day itself, the weekly inspection of both quarters and men came round. The amount of cleaning done every Sunday was something awful. Guns had to be taken apart and made to look better than when they left the armory, brasses to be polished, shoes and equipments blacked, and bunks and barracks put in perfect order. This was varied occasionally by a knapsack inspection, which consisted in standing in the hot sun for an hour or two, our knapsacks on our backs, apparently filled with all our worldly goods; but appearances are sometimes deceitful, and so were our knapsacks, but if they only looked full, we were perfectly content.

In the afternoon we formed a hollow square and had a regular New England service, with a clear, practical sermon from the chaplain, finishing the exercises with the Doxology, in which both band and regiment were wont to join. The day closed with the usual dress-parade and a prayer meeting in the evening conducted by the chaplain.

Thanksgiving Day being close at hand, most of us began to busy ourselves making preparations for a proper observance of the day. Mysterious trips to town, frequent visits to Aunt Gatsy's, and a great scarcity of ready money were the most observable features. Thanksgiving eve arrived at last, clear and cold, and after the labors for the day were ended, we built a famous large fire in our barracks, and long after taps remained grouped about it, talking of home and former times in old Massachusetts when this anniversary came round. One by one the men dropped off to bed, until but four of us remained, when one of our number proposed whist by fire-light. The cards were quickly produced, and an impromptu lunch of crackers and cheese, apples and lemonade, contributed from our private stores, and there we played till the waning light of the fire warned us that our supply of wood was exhausted, whereupon we crept noiselessly to our bunks, not daring to think how soon the inexorable reveille would break in upon our slumbers.

After a sermon in the morning from the chaplain, in accordance with the good old custom of New England, the day was given as a holiday, and thanks to Old Aunty, our little party of six sat down to a repast which would not have disgraced any board in the land, and all agreed that we had rarely enjoyed a dinner more.

About this time, Colonel Codman received orders to detail two companies for special service, and for several days quite an excitement prevailed as to which they were to be. The question was settled by the departure, on the first of December, of Company C, for Morehead City, and on the next day, of Company G, under command of Lieutenant Thayer, for Fort Macon. Several of the officers and many of the men were also detached from the regiment about this same time. Captain Murdock, of Company G, went on to Colonel Amory's staff, as aide, and Lieutenant Dewson as Brigade Quarter-Master, his place being filled by Lieutenant Emmons, of Company E. Lieutenants Richardson, of Company A, and Blagden, of Company I, went into the Signal Corps, and never rejoined their command. The men were variously distributed, some on signal service, many as clerks at the various headquarters, assistants in the hospitals, teamsters, etc., thus materially weakening the regiment in point of numbers by these heavy details.

The first time the men went out on picket they made preparations enough for an expedition, and bade good-bye as if at the very least they were sure for Richmond, instead of simply bivouacing for a night across the Trent. The truth is, that so far from resembling that on the Potomac, picketing was with us rather a pleasant diversion than otherwise. There were six stations, all on the other side the Trent; the outermost station directly on the river, the others at intervals along the road. Each station was under command of a corporal; and the guard, equipped with blankets and rations, went out one morning and were relieved the next. Intended as a safeguard, and rather for practice than from any real expectation of an approach of the enemy in that direction, we had nevertheless, one night, an example of the practical working and great advantage of the picket guard. One of the outermost station fired upon what in the darkness he took to be a body of rebels, and the alarm was immediately communicated to the camp guard. The drummers beat the long roll, and in a very short time the whole camp was aroused, the regiment in line, and in readiness for the enemy whenever he saw fit to come. It was well for us, however, that we did not wait till he did come, but after standing shivering in the cold night air for about an hour, went back to the barracks, otherwise we might have stood there to this day.

The road to Newbern was considerably altered in appearance by the arrival of General Wessel's division of New York and Pennsylvania troops from Suffolk, Va., which encamped about half a mile from us; and as every day brought news of fresh arrivals, it was very evident that some movement was on foot in our department. Rumor was very busy about these times, and the camp was full of reports and stories. Charleston, Wilmington, and even Richmond itself were named as our destination. Nothing was thought, talked, or dreamt of, but the probable expedition, and if it had ended in talk, our loss under the influence of undue excitement would have been very heavy. But about the eighth of December, our feelings were somewhat relieved by the reading of marching orders to the regiment, three days being given to prepare for the march.

The note of preparation sounded through the camp, and all was bustle and confusion. Knapsacks were filled to overflowing with all our worldly possessions, and stowed in a schooner which came up the river to receive them, so that in case of an attack or fire in our absence, they at least might be secure, and indeed such good care did those on board take, that they have kept some of our things to this day.

It fell to my lot to be detailed on picket the last day, and so entrusting my property to the tender mercies of my chum, the guard started for the other side of the river, wholly ignorant as to whether they were to be left behind or not. However, having three old whalers from Nantucket as companions in misery, the day passed away very quickly, listening to their tales of sea life, its pleasures and dangers, but above all, its superiority to the life of a soldier. But my special wonder and admiration was excited by witnessing the relish with which they devoured the salt junk at their dinner, actually preferring it to fresh beef, to me a most unaccountable taste.

The night was bright and clear, and the moonlight glimmering through the tops of the old pine trees, lit up the scene just around us, but deepened the blackness of the shadows which hid themselves in the surrounding forest. As we sat round the smouldering embers of the deadened fire, wondering as to our probable fortune, whether the morrow would behold us on the march with the regiment, or ignominiously left behind to guard the camp, our doubts and fears were set at rest by the arrival of the lieutenant of the guard. He informed us that at ten o'clock the pickets were to be taken in, and at that hour we were to proceed to the barracks as quietly as possible. The hour came at last, and rolling up our blankets and shouldering our guns, before long we were once more in camp.

During our absence all our goods had been removed, rations distributed, and ammunition given out; while in anticipation of the hard work before them, all were sleeping quietly in their bunks, some poor fellows for the last time. Making all our preparations for the morrow as speedily as possible, we crawled upon the boards, and soon forgot our trials in the land of dreams.

BATTLE OF KINSTON.

CHAPTER IV.

ON THE MARCH.

THE first tap of the drum at early morn of the eleventh instant, aroused us with that faint consciousness of something important before us, with which the sleeper always wakens on the day of some long-expected event. The last preparations were gone through, blankets rolled, canteens filled and lost straps found, while hurry and confusion reigned supreme in the various quarters.

At last, everything was in readiness, and as the impatient drums sounded the assembly call, we marched out on the parade-ground as if for a review. The line was formed, with the pioneers in advance, and with band playing and colors flying, the 45th started on its first expedition, their hearts beating high with hope and enthusiasm. On every side of us trooped our contraband camp followers, laden down with all manner of strange things, such as the ingenuity of an inexperienced officer's mind could suggest as likely to contribute to his wants and comfort, from a cooking-stove to a shoe-brush. The two miles of sandy road which lay between the camp and the town, served in a measure to dampen the ardor of some of the more demonstrative ones, and more than one armor vest, which the kind but injudicious care of friends had provided, was left to rest by the wayside before the end of those first two miles.

On reaching the city we found the streets crowded with troops of every description, infantry, cavalry and artillery, massed together in almost endless confusion. But after two or three hours delay, the different commanders began to find their proper positions in the line of march, and about eleven o'clock of the eleventh of December, the long column moved forward.

Past Fort Totten, out on the Trent road, the line for a short time presented an orderly appearance. But soon there was a bridge to cross, a great puddle to pick your way around or go splashing through, as inclination directed; then a stream, whose bridge was a log on one side, admitting only of single file, the water, yellow and dirty, looking suspiciously deep for wading. The unfortunates in the rear had to make up for these delays by frequent double-quick, until at length all distinction, not merely of regiments but also of companies, had disappeared. The march subsided into a mere race between individuals, all making for some unknown object ahead, at the highest rate of speed. On! On! Will the column never halt, or have the advance suddenly become possessed of cork legs, which like those in the song, will never stop, thought the poor fellows on this first morning of their march, when those fell enemies of the soldier, sore feet, lame backs and aching limbs, became clamorous for their victims.

At last, came the halt for dinner, and most of us experienced a full realization of the blessedness of rest, while our hard-tack and coffee was like the milk and honey to the Jews. But time and our leaders are inexorable, and already the lengthening shadows reprove delay, so once more the hurrying, tearing pace begins. But now our colonel has made a wise rule, that on passing any obstacle tending to delay the rear, the head of the regiment shall halt until the last company has passed. This prevents the recurrence of intervals so disheartening for those in the rear to see opening before them, and requiring an extra effort to make up the lost space.

We had little leisure that first day to examine the country about us, but every now and then a deserted house, the forlorn, desolate appearance of those still occupied, and the looks of the miserable, half-starved creatures, who, with undisguised hatred in their eyes, stood gazing on the moving tide of Yankee soldiery, gave but too good evidence that the iron hand of war had been laid very heavily upon this people. Truly, they were suffering for the sins of their leaders, and their hatred of the Northern troops was not to be wondered at, when they slaughtered their cattle, seized their horses, plundered their poultry yards, and even entered their houses and snatched the food from their mouths, without so much as a "by your leave."

Our progress became slower as evening drew near, and several times the column was obliged to halt to allow time for the rebuilding of bridges which were destroyed by the enemy on our approach. Darkness soon enveloped us, but the weary train still pressed on. At last, however, our hearts were gladdened by the distant gleam of light flashing in the horizon, for we soon learned that it was caused by the fires of our advance guard.

Our burden grew lighter as we hurried forward, refreshed by the sight, and when at last, descending a hill, we emerged from the woods which skirted its brow, a scene burst upon our startled vision which, in its picturesque beauty, almost repaid us for the long and weary way we had traversed before reaching it.

A large field, stretching for nearly a mile to the left of the road, was streaked with long rows of fires, made of dry pitch-pine rails, and as the figures flitted about midst the fires, weird shadows were thrown against the black woods and sky beyond. It seemed like a glimpse into some other world, and when our regiment, and the many others in the rear, reached the fairy spot, and added their fires to the grand illumination, the heavens became red with flame.

Most of us were through with work for that night, and had no harder task to perform than to collect a few rails, boil some coffee, and after supper make ourselves comfortable for the night. But all were not so fortunate, for some were detailed for picket duty, and as for the poor pioneers, the enemy, in their retreat, had laid out several hours' work for them, by felling trees across the road for nearly half a mile, rendering it impassable for the artillery. The choppers had almost completed their job, and had left one huge old pine, beyond which, preparatory to commencing the attack, they had built a roaring fire in the middle of the road. Suddenly, up rode one of the 3d N. Y. Cavalry, leading a second horse, laden with a foraged bag of grain. He was very impatient to rejoin his comrades, encamped some distance in advance of the main body, and all advice to wait for the removal of the obstacle proved of no avail. Wheeling about, and riding back a few rods, he started the two horses on the full gallop, leaped the tree, directly into the fire, dashed on, and was quickly lost in the thick darkness beyond.

Refreshed by our night's rest, we were roused at early dawn by the reveille-call of the bugle, and soon the whole camp was astir. Breakfast, which, like both the other meals, consisted of hard-tack and coffee, except when a successful foraging tour increased our commissariat, was soon disposed of, and we started on the second day's march. Wading a broad stream, at the very outset, relieved us from all fear of wetting our feet, and enabled us to travel regardless of mud and water. We were all becoming more accustomed to the work before us, though whether that proved of any practical benefit in rendering the labor easier, is still an open question.

As we had loaded our guns before starting that morning, we confidently expected to meet the enemy before the close of the day; but, though occasional firing was to be heard at the front, the skirmishing of our advance with the rear of the enemy, nothing of the foe was to be seen, except some prisoners captured by the cavalry, several of them wounded. It was a sad spectacle, the sight of the poor rebels in their forlorn condition, so gaunt and filthy, most miserably clad, and above all, wounded and captive. The horrors of war were indeed becoming a dread reality and no longer mere printed words. Another sad sight was to see the men straggling. Poor fellows, who, reduced by fever in the summer, and but scarcely dismissed from the hospital, lined the road, utterly exhausted and unable to drag one limb after the other. Others, from our own ranks, unaccustomed to such hard work, and used up by the march of the day previous, were compelled to fall out and rest, after an hour or two of vain attempts to keep up with the hurrying crowd.

The country grew pleasanter as we advanced, and food seemed much more plentiful; the woods swarmed with wild pigs; cattle and poultry were quite abundant, and occasionally a hive of honey was discovered, and quickly dismounted and robbed, regardless of its fiery occupants. Halts were more frequent that day, and as the camping-ground was earlier reached, the bivouac was so much the more comfortable. The night was quite cold, and the ground stiff and frozen in the morning, but we soon thawed ourselves out before the rekindled fires. Some of the improvident ones awoke to a sense of their folly, in having emptied their haversacks at the end of the second day, not having considered the simple problem that if three days rations are eaten in two days, the third day they must either beg or starve.

We had a very easy day's work on the thirteenth, for after marching a few hours, firing commenced in the front, and orders came for us to hurry forward, as the enemy had made a stand. As we pressed eagerly onward, the cry was passed along from the rear, of "Give way, right and left, for artillery!" We were marching through a long, level stretch of pine forest, and as the men fell back on each side of the road, we could see the batteries approaching in the distance. As they drew near, the leader shouted, "Gallop!" and on they came, the horses on the full run, the guns rattling and jumping, the men clinging to their seats for dear life, to prevent being dismounted by some extra jounce, but smiling as if going to parade. Cheer after cheer greeted each successive piece as it rushed through our ranks on to the front, and we all felt sure that with such support we could brave any foe.

Leaving the main road, the regiment filed into a cleared space, where the advance had halted and was drawn up in line of battle with the rest of the brigade. The skirmishers advanced and disappeared in the woods, and we awaited anxiously our orders to move; but after a few shots from cavalry and skirmishers, the enemy fell back, leaving in our possession two small pieces of artillery. It was decided to halt for the night, to give the men a good rest, as our proximity to Kinston made a fight the next day almost inevitable.

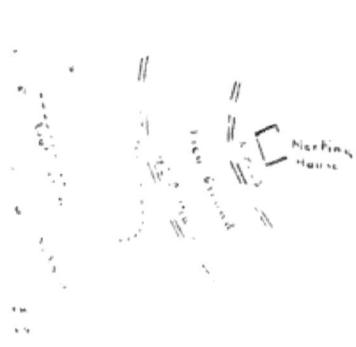
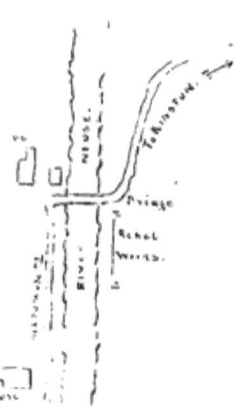

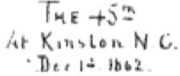

The 45th
At Kinston N.C.
Dec 1st 1862.

CHAPTER V.

OUR BATTLES.

THE quiet afternoon and long night's rest refreshed us most wonderfully, and we woke the next morning, Sunday, the fourteenth, free from all fatigue. It was a bright, beautiful day, and we broke camp in high spirits, ready for whatever might happen, and yet with no conception of the dread realities actually before us, and in which we were to enact a part.

After marching two or three miles, firing once more commenced at the front, and hurrying on, the regiment was halted at the corner of a road which ran directly to the river Neuse. Presently, a section of artillery arrived, and passing into a field just before us, began to shell the woods.

As we waited there, momentarily expecting to enter the fight already begun, one of our number, amid the roar of artillery and occasional roll of musketry, began the hymn, forever associated in the minds of those present with that scene, "Ye Christian Heroes go Proclaim," in which we all joined. It was his last song upon earth, but how nobly did he earn the title of "Christian Hero," and what death more glorious than with such words yet lingering on his lips, to freely surrender his life at the altar of his country's liberty. His name will ever be cherished with love and reverence by all who knew him, and we can rejoice with his friends who mourn his loss, that he is enjoying his fit reward, an immortal crown of glory.

Soon the order came for the 45th to advance; so, marching by the right flank, we left the road and entered the woods, passing directly in front of the battery, and most unfortunately in its range. Before notice could be given to the officer in command, two successive shells had killed three of our number, besides slightly wounding others. It was a sad omen with which to enter the fight, but on we pushed and soon faced to the front and advanced, deployed as skirmishers.

We quickly found ourselves in the midst of a regular North Carolina swamp, which in ordinary times would be considered impenetrable. Mud and water waist deep, how much deeper none stopped to see, roots to trip the careless foot, briers innumerable to make havoc with our clothes, to say nothing of an occasional stray bullet, which, finding its way through the trees, whistled over our heads, and contributed to the pleasantness of the position. But it needed more than mud and water, or even a stray bullet, to check us, and so on we crept, crawled and waded, the bullets becoming thicker as we advanced, until we conquered the swamp and gained a position where the ground rose slightly towards the enemy, and was thinly covered with young oaks and underbrush. Here we quickly obeyed the order "Lie down!"

The regiment formed in a sort of semi-circle around the edge of the woods, but the line was too much extended to be efficient in a charge, as we soon found. We retained this position for about an hour amid an unceasing storm of bullets, shot and shell, which, thanks to the elevation of the ground, passed in a great measure just above our heads and riddled the trees in our rear. Too many, however, found a resting place in a soldier's body, and the dead and wounded lay in every direction. We fired at will, as we found opportunity, our regiment, the 10th Connecticut and 103d Pennsylvania, who following in our footsteps had gained the same position, all lying together, regardless of company or regiment.

At last, the order came to fix bayonets, and then to charge. The left wing, together with the Connecticut and Pennsylvania troops, sprang to their feet, and with a loud cry broke from the cover. At the same moment, the enemy gave way and retreated posthaste across the bridge which leads to Kinston. But the extended line of our regiment, scattered as it was through the woods, and the impossibility of conveying an order in the din of battle, simultaneously to all parts of the line, prevented a united movement, and those who had received and obeyed the order to charge were soon halted, to enable the scattered ranks to reunite.

But the day was won, and the rebels, in full retreat across the river, received an occasional reminder in the shape of a shell from our guns, which hastened their speed till it became a run.

We discovered, on emerging from the woods, that the enemy had been sheltered behind fences on both sides of the road. This enabled them to concentrate upon us a cross fire. An old barn-like church had also served to protect them in a measure. It was perforated with holes of all sizes, from that of the Minie-ball to the one caused by the thirty-two-pound shell. Dead bodies lay scattered about the floor, and our surgeons immediately appropriated it for a hospital.

After a time, we marched down the road to the river, and turning down the Neuse road in the direction of Newbern, went into camp a short distance from the bridge. Expecting to bivouac here, we commenced our preparations for the night. Some of us, meantime, returned to the swamp to recover our blankets, overcoats and haversacks, cast aside at the commencement of the fight, and were fortunate enough to recover most of them. The dead and wounded lay scattered through the woods, and with sad hearts we rejoined our comrades, thankful that our lives had been spared. But our day's work was by no means ended, for scarcely had our party returned to the camping-ground, when the order came to fall in, and off we started across the bridge, which the rebels had made a vain attempt to burn in their retreat, and marched along the banks of the Neuse, till we reached the town of Kinston.

The strategy which enabled General Foster to win this battle as easily as he did, was apparent when we came to understand the nature of the country and the works of the enemy. The rebels had evidently expected us to advance by the Neuse road, which runs along the riverside; for, some distance from the bridge, a strong earth-work had been thrown up directly across the road, flanked on one side by a pond, on the other by a swamp. A long earth-work had also been erected on the Kinston side of the river, commanding both roads and the bridge.

The road taken by General Foster rendered the first mentioned work wholly useless, and the garrison was compelled to abandon it to prevent their separation from the main command. The road taken by the main body of our force, makes a bend, which brings it to the bridge at right angles to the river. Nearly a quarter of a mile from this bend, a small cross-road connects with the Neuse road, thus enclosing a square, in which the enemy made their stand, compelled to fight on what, to them, was the farther side of the river, and thus they were made dependent on the bridge for a means of retreat.

The plan was to divide our force, the main body keeping straight forward, towards the bridge, and thus bring on a general engagement, while meantime, a strong force was sent down the cross-road, in order to gain possession of the bridge, and so cut off their sole means of escape. This manœuvre was only partially successful, as the rebels, discovering their imminent danger, gave way before the flanking force had reached the bridge. However, some five hundred prisoners were captured, as it was, and eleven cannon fell into our hands, to say nothing of small arms and commissary stores.

Some seven thousand of the enemy, under command of General Evans, were engaged, and not many more on our side, as many of our regiments took no active part in the battle. When compared with many other battles of the war, it was a mere skirmish; but veterans from the seven-days fight before Richmond, from Roanoke, and from Newbern, were unanimous in pronouncing the fire that day, to have been sharper than was experienced by them in any former battle. General Foster, in his despatch, speaks of the "terrible fire" to which we were exposed.

Kinston is rather a pretty place, regularly laid out, well shaded, and altogether very New England like. It is built directly on the Neuse, whose banks are high and steep at this point. We marched through the town, and halted at the outskirts, on the line of the railroad, which runs from Newbern to Goldsboro, and on which most of the enemy made good their retreat.

After the camp had been selected, and our goods and chattels deposited, the band gave an impromptu concert, in honor of the victory, after which most of us started on a foraging expedition, seeking what we might devour. In this quest we were eminently successful. Our mess supped on broiled chicken and apple-jack, and others fared even more sumptuously. A large quantity of tobacco was also discovered and speedily confiscated.

Hardly had we finished supper, and laid ourselves out for the night, when the order came for four companies to "fall in," and patrol the town. A house in the middle of the town had been fired, and as the flames had extended to one or two of the surrounding buildings, there was a fair prospect of seeing the whole place in ashes before morning, unless the progress of the fire was arrested. Fortunately there were enough firemen to check any further spread of the mischief, and it devolved upon us to pass the greater half of the night patrolling the streets, preventing all disorder, and returning stragglers to their regiments. We found one fellow in a most happy frame of mind, seated in a horseless chaise, evidently enjoying his ride intensely, and urging on the imaginary steed, as if on a race track, apple-jack, without question, having got the better of him.

The moon came out in full splendor, to light us on our weary pilgrimage, as we traversed the streets back and forth, round and round. The captain occasionally coming to a halt, some of us employed the time by taking a nap on the sidewalk, or in the road, just as it happened. A colored gentleman accompanied us during part of our wanderings, showing off the place, pointing out the slave market, and other objects of interest. However, our desire for a more intimate acquaintance with the town was not so great but that we were ready to return to camp, somewhere in the small hours, and wrap up in our blankets for a short nap, after our day's work.

We were up bright and early the next morning, and to our surprise, and the enemy's as well, Kinston was abandoned, and the river recrossed. The rear guard destroyed the bridge, which had cost us so much effort to save the day before, and we started once more in the direction of Goldsboro. It was very warm and dusty, and the march long and wearisome, but the country grew pleasanter the further inland we advanced, and the plantations appeared much more flourishing, so that we were more than usually rejoiced to reach the camp that night, and rest after our two days of hard work.

After marching three or four miles the next morning, Tuesday, the 16th, the boom of cannon, now quite familiar, was heard in the distance, and orders came for the 45th to hasten forward to the scene of action.

The road runs for some distance parallel to the river, through a large clearing, and then turns abruptly towards a bridge which spans the Neuse, leading to the town of Whitehall. The land rises to some height on the left side of the road, the brow of the hill being thinly covered with forest trees, while on the right it slopes to the wooded bank of the river.

On the approach of our cavalry advance, the previous night, the rebels had crossed the river, destroying the bridge in their retreat, and the fighting was now going on at this point, the apparent object being to rebuild the bridge, and cross the river. The part taken in this fight by our regiment was rather passive than active, but none the less trying for that reason.

A portion of a New York battery, being put in position on the rise of the hill, we were ordered to their support; so, marching along the road till opposite the battery, we formed in line of battle, and then lay down, facing the river, and not many rods distant from it. Our situation was anything but an agreeable one, for not only did the rebel shot and bullets fall thick around us, but the shell from our own guns behind, passed so near as to render a recumbent posture very desirable. An hour passed in this condition, without firing a gun, seemed, from the very inaction, much more like two or three; but at length the order was passed along the line to fall back to the other side of the road. So, crawling through, or scrambling over the fence which separated us from the field, we took up a new position, two or three rods further back, and directly the 3d Rhode Island Battery came thundering down the road, and unlimbering on the spot we had just vacated, began to pour a deadly fire across the river. While we occupied this position, our gallant Color Sergeant, Theodore Parkman, was struck in the head by a fragment of a shell, and almost instantly killed. But before the colors fell to the ground they were seized by the colonel himself, and though a mark for the deadly missiles of the sharp-shooters, which whistled close around him, he supported them till relieved by one of the color-guard.

It is true we accomplished the destruction of a gunboat, which was in process of construction at this place, but all this apparent effort to cross the river was merely a feint to occupy the attention of the enemy, and thereby cover a raid of the cavalry upon the Goldsboro and Wilmington Railroad. It was most successful, for a battalion of the 3d New York having struck the road at Mt. Olive Station, took the people wholly by surprise. They came upon a crowd of passengers waiting for the train, which was, however, unavoidably detained on that day, at least, as they destroyed the track and telegraph for some miles, rejoining the main command without the loss of a man.

We marched on some hours after the fight was over, finding the country much more hilly, and decidedly pleasanter. The latter part of the day, a few of us, wearying of the monotony of the march, started ahead on our own account, passing regiment after regiment. An occasional meeting with old friends among the Massachusetts troops, with whom we rehearsed the events of the past two or three days, created quite a pleasant diversion, and relieved to a great extent the tedium of the way.

CHAPTER VI.

THE RETURN.

UP to the last day's advance, our brigade had been one of the first in line of march, but that last day the 45th was detailed as guard over the baggage train. We were consequently prevented from participating in or even witnessing the battle at the bridge where the railroad crosses the Neuse, a short distance from the town of Goldsboro, which resulted in the destruction of the bridge.

Our regiment was drawn up in line by the roadside, awaiting orders, when General Foster and his staff came riding up from the scene of action. The general himself announced the successful accomplishment of the object of the expedition, which good news was received with loud cheers, followed by a salute from the band.

At night-fall, on the return march, we had just reached the bivouac of the previous night, when firing was once more heard in the direction of Goldsboro, and presently an orderly dashed up with orders for us to hurry back, as an attack in force had been made by the enemy on our retiring column. This was anything but agreeable, as we were anticipating a good supper and a quiet night; but war is inexorable, and so we faced about and hurried off on the back-track. At the end of four miles, the firing ceased, and soon word came that we were not wanted, and might once more turn our faces homeward.

By this time it was quite dark, and the men very naturally felt cross and tired, and did not execute some order of the colonel as promptly as he thought right. Whereupon, he treated us on the spot to a drill in the manual, full fifteen minutes long. Our way back to camp was lit up by the blazing fences and pines which had caught from the fires made by the troops along the road at the various halting places, and presented a beautiful appearance, yet at the same time the scene was not wholly free from danger, as the burning trees were falling in all directions. The sky was red with the blaze, and it was a grand sight to watch the fire creep slowly up the trunks of the old dead pines, towering high above the other trees, and gradually envelope them in one sheet of flame.

The next day we were fully initiated into the mysteries, as well as duties, of baggage guard. Four men were detailed to a wagon, two on each side, and off start the teams, most of them empty, at a rate of about ten or twelve miles an hour. Running beside the wagon was rather severe exercise, and sitting with the driver almost an impossibility, strict orders being given by the wagon-master to allow no one to ride. There was, therefore, nothing to be done but let them go their own gait, or else climb up and cling to the inverted trough, used in feeding the horses, which hangs at the back of most army wagons. The wise ones chose this latter course, and by constant practice acquired great expertness in getting on and off while

at full speed. At length, by judiciously walking up
the hills, occasionally presenting ourselves at the front
of the wagon to show the driver we were on hand, and
assisting in watering the horses, we worked on his
feelings to such an extent that a seat by his side
crowned our efforts. Our good fortune was, however,
but short-lived, for the wagon-master, on discovering
our comfortable position, most unceremoniously ejected
us therefrom, leaving us to finish the journey on foot,
for which kind act he has our grateful maledictions.
Rations began to run very low about this time, and
the houses on the road were very thoroughly searched
and stripped of all things eatable.

Our column presented a most singular appearance
on the return march, for each one seemed to be his
own commander, and all thoughts of company or regiment were wholly thrown aside. A most motley
appearance we must have presented. Here comes
one mounted on a nice horse, with a halter for his
bridle, a blanket for his saddle; another has found
a home-made cart, into which, by dint of rope and
strap, he has fastened some old Rosinante, a perfect
match for the vehicle, and thus rides in state in his
own carriage. There is a mule, which in its obstinacy
causes the rider much more trouble, and consumes
more time, than an equal amount of walking; while a
strange crowd on foot, their faces black with the accu-
mulation of nine days' dirt, armed with plunder of
every shape and kind, from a sauce-pan to a feather
pillow, hurry along, each one suiting his own convenience and acknowledging no other leader.

It was a pretty hungry time for a day or two, and
for one forty-eight hours but four hard-tack to a man

were issued by the quartermaster, and those who were unsuccessful in their foraging went very hungry. The officers fared no better than the men, as the following incident certainly bespeaks a most sharp and craving appetite. After we had gone into camp, on one of these nights of scarcity, a lieutenant in our regiment was prowling supperless about the staff headquarters, and in the course of his wanderings came upon a contraband making a supper off the remains of the mess-table. Called away for a moment, he laid down his dish, leaving on it a bone not thoroughly picked; but alas for the poor darkey! when he returned, the bone was gone, and his feast was over, while the lieutenant alone remained to tell the story.

Our expedition had its pleasures as well as its pains, and though perhaps not as numerous, yet they were all the choicer for their rarity. Passing through a strange country, where houses and people differed from what we were accustomed to, every object was novel and full of interest. Foraging was full of charm, not only because of the excitement it afforded, but from its utter lawlessness. It was something so entirely opposed to all civilized proceedings, to boldly enter a house and demand and take something to eat, or deliberately walk off with a goose or chicken, without so much as "by your leave" to the owner.

Then this wild, out-of-door life; lying close to old Mother Earth, with the blue canopy of heaven for our covering; the merry camp-fires, surrounded after a day of toil by a circle of weary but contented faces, busy preparing supper. The more enterprising ones, who had been successful in their foraging, cooking their chicken or hoe-cake, or perhaps a bit of bacon filched from some smoke-house, while the unlucky or lazy ones have only to boil their coffee and make a meal off of hard-tack, when they have any. Every little while a shout of dismay is heard as some luckless wight stumbles over the end of the long rail which stretches out into the darkness, but on whose fire-end are nicely poised two or three cups of coffee, almost ready to drink, and their unfortunate owner sees the precious contents spilled into the fire. It was no small trial of temper, after going perhaps half a mile at the end of a wearisome march to fill your canteen with water, to lose both water and coffee by the awkwardness of some stupid fellow. The only equally provoking accident is, to have your blanket-straps give way while wading a mud-puddle, and see the blankets fall into the mud.

The fine weather, with which we were favored, was another pleasant feature of the expedition. The nights were cold, to be sure, but the air was clear and bracing, and we were spared all the discomforts of a stormy campaign. We learnt more of the true character of our comrades also, for nothing brings out the real worth of a man more than such an experience. Some, who had been very stout and bold-hearted in the anticipation, sank utterly under the reality; while others, from whom little had been expected, now appeared as lively and active as if on a pleasure excursion, and occasionally you would see a noble-hearted fellow carrying two guns, or an extra set of blankets, but for whose kindly assistance some poor fellow would have given up in utter despair.

One of the saddest sights of the march was the great number of stragglers. We read in the newspapers of so many stragglers picked off by guerillas, or captured and missing, and one naturally supposes that these unlucky ones have wilfully strayed from the command, and suffered the penalty for their carelessness and disobedience. But what is the reality? As the column goes hurrying by, you catch a glimpse of a pale face lying by the road-side, faint and weary; a few steps farther on, one with his shoes off, bathing his blistered feet; here is a poor fellow whose summer has been spent in hospital, sick of a fever, and whose little stock of strength is soon exhausted; these are the stragglers who reach the camp long after the others have made themselves comfortable for the night, and, after a restless night, they start off the next morning with a like prospect before them, until human endurance can hold out no longer.

On the tenth night we found ourselves but eight miles from Newbern, and the next morning we started for the barracks with happy, thankful hearts. About noon of the eleventh day, after a march of more than one hundred and fifty miles, a motley crew, some with faces which had known no water during our absence, and all unshaven, tattered and torn, we once more set foot in Camp Amory on the Trent. After the luxury of a bath and change of clothes, we had a great treat in the budget of letters and pile of boxes which had been awaiting our return, suggestive of numberless feasts, to make up for the scanty fare on the march. Such was our first experience of the stern realities of war. Out of the eight companies who went on the expedition, seventeen men were killed and sixty wounded, — one in every ten of the command.

We soon fell into the old routine of camp life, the

regimental library furnishing a supply of reading for the evening hours, and when reading and writing failed, whist was always on hand, a never-failing resource. Not long after our return to camp, the regiment, in common with many others which were quartered in barracks, was visited by a deadly malaria, which carried off several brave fellows who had escaped the dangers of the march only to fall victims to disease. As one after another was stricken down, and in a few short hours lay cold and still in death, a shadow fell upon us all, for none could tell whose turn would come next. We entered the service with the dangers of the battle-field distinctly before us, but this was a foe against which mortal might was powerless. There is a glory in a death in battle, but equal honor and equal praise is due to him who suffers for his country's good in a different way, and at her call gives up his life on the sick-bed, with a heroism equal to those who shed their life-blood in the fight. All honor and praise be to both.

Being exempted from drill the day after guard duty, we used to make little excursions about the country; through the woods on the opposite side of the river, hunting after brier-root to make pipes, and also to collect logs for the barrack fire; to the old brick house, once the mansion-house of the plantation upon which our camps were situated, now torn down, and the bricks converted into chimneys and ovens for the barracks, while the surrounding grove has fallen before the axes of the pioneer. Still farther off, stood the block-house on Brice's Creek, the outpost in this direction, a favorite resort, while near by was a signal-tower, from which a fine view of Newbern and the vicinity could be obtained.

Christmas came, marked by an absence of drill, and an extra dinner, followed by the New Year's day, so memorable on account of the Emancipation Proclamation that day given to the world. But a very important event, and one long looked for, occurred early in January, which sent a thrill of joy throughout the department,—that was the arrival of the paymaster and our first pay-day. He had been coming every day for many weeks; and some regiments had not been paid for more than six months, and their families were suffering for want of this dearly-earned money. But come he did, and a happy set of faces filled the long line as it filed by his table, receiving the first earning in Uncle Sam's service. But transcendent in his joy was the sutler, who, seated by the paymaster, eyed the crisp bank-notes, and speculated how soon they would find their way into his rapacious maw.

HARDTACK AND COFFEE.

BLOCK HOUSE.

RESERVE PICKET STATION.

CHAPTER VII.

A TRIP TO TRENTON.

WE had but fairly settled down to the old story of drill and parade, our lameness healed, and the excitement of the scenes through which we had so lately passed somewhat allayed, when rumors of another expedition began to float about the camp. These were vague at first, but increased in strength from day to day, until we became convinced of their truth by the announcement at dress-parade of the order to be in readiness on a certain day, with three days' rations ready cooked. Having learned wisdom by experience, we understood better how to prepare for a march. My first care was to procure a body-guard in the shape of a stout contraband youth, to relieve me of my blankets and look after my interests generally; the next was to make some provision for the inner man, additional to that of government, which had failed us before in the hour of need. Thanks to a box from home, a ham, not quite demolished, made an excellent substitute for salt junk, and a package of rice also found its way into our haversack. This possessed the double advantage of furnishing great nourishment and occupying but a small space in the bag.

Several gentlemen from Boston, who had arrived shortly before our departure, had an opportunity of seeing the regiment leave camp on an expedition. Our force consisted of one brigade of infantry, — 1st Brigade, 1st Division, 18th Army Corps, — a squadron of cavalry, with a small howitzer, and a section of artillery, all under command of Colonel Amory, our brigade commander. Two or three unsuccessful attempts to start had been made, as a storm prevented, but Saturday, the 17th, dawned, a clear, cold January day, and shortly after breakfast we left camp and were soon fairly on our way. While awaiting the arrival of the detachment of cavalry and artillery which was to accompany us, a very amusing scene occurred, in the shape of an extempore drill by some of the contrabands — our camp followers — under the leadership of a deep-voiced darkey, whose orders were, to say the least, remarkable: such as, " In three ranks count twos, Right smart, Git!" while the execution of these manœuvres was, if possible, even more ludicrous than the orders themselves.

The first day's march was through an uninteresting section of country, very sparsely settled, and more hilly than any we had passed through before. The march was quite reasonable, bringing us to the village of Pollocksville, distant a little more than twelve miles from Newbern. The town comprised only about half-a-dozen houses, remarkable solely for their homeliness. The place, however, once boasted a private school of some pretensions. The large white building, not far from the town, standing a little distance from the road, immediately attracted our attention, and a halt occurring just then, we made an inspection.

Some circulars were found setting forth the merits of the school, and advising parents not to let the distractions of war interfere with the education of their children. But teachers and scholars had alike disappeared long since, and the building alone remained, forlorn and desolate.

As we entered the village, two or three men were seen in the distance, and some of the cavalry immediately dashed off at full run in hot pursuit, but, having gained the woods, they made good their escape. The half-dozen houses were mostly deserted, and extensive levies were made upon them for boards, which, covered with a sufficient number of weeds and stalks, made a bed fit for a king, and almost too luxurious for a soldier. Taking it quite leisurely the next morning, as some trees felled across the road caused delay, we started *en route* for Trenton, leaving part of our force to guard the baggage-train which remained at Pollocksville.

This day's march was, without exception, the pleasantest in all our experience. We were not hurried, as always before, and had some opportunity to look about and see the country through which we were passing. This section had been very little disturbed by raiding armies; the plantations grew larger the further we advanced, and the houses had a very comfortable, hospitable appearance, but as foraging was strictly forbidden, a close inspection was out of the question. For some distance the road skirted a cypress swamp, a most desolate, gloomy spot, the old trees, hoary with the long gray moss which hung in festoons from every limb, and surrounded with slimy water, suggestive of snakes and horrible reptiles, — secure retreat for the fugitive.

Our command entered Trenton without opposition, a small force of the enemy retreating in hot haste on the approach of our cavalry. After going into camp and disposing of our luggage, we wandered about the town, seeking what we might devour, but finding little to reward us for our pains. The town is prettily situated on the river Trent, but the houses and people were forlorn and dirty enough. The post-office was ransacked, but little besides recruiting bills was to be found. One great object in coming to this place was to destroy the bridge across the Trent, and so prevent any advance on Newbern from this direction. Our arrival was a happy event for the slaves in and about the town, and they spent the night in preparation for their exodus from the land of bondage. The bridge burned, we started on the back road, accompanied by a long train of contrabands. A mill at the entrance of the town was fired to prevent the use of its timbers for the reconstruction of the bridge, and some one at the same time let on the water, and as the groan of the machinery rose above the roar of the flames, we could imagine it some huge creature awaiting in agony a fiery death.

The next night we spent at our old camp at Pollocksville, and very narrowly escaped quite a serious disaster; for the grass in the large field where we encamped, being quite high and dry, took fire, and burned with such violence that it was only by great exertion that we saved our guns and traps from destruction. With replenished haversacks, we made a fresh start the next morning in the direction of Onslow Court House, following in the tracks of the cavalry, who had started the previous afternoon with two pieces of artillery. Early in the afternoon we reached a place called Young's Cross Roads, where the cavalry had captured an army wagon and a few prisoners. Here we bivouacked, and as the sky looked threatening, made preparations for a stormy night, for we were to await the return of the cavalry, or, if needful, go on to their support.

While hard at work, making as good shelter as possible with boards and rubber blankets, round came the orderly with the detail for picket duty, our name among the rest; so, dropping rails and boards, and once more donning our harness, we reported with our squad to the officer of the guard. The road we were detached to guard led to some mills, — Packard's, by name, — and every little while three or four men were dropped off under charge of a corporal, until the lieutenant announced that the next station would be the reserve, with a guard of twenty. Such of our company as were detailed on guard, were among this lucky number, and we quickly set to work to prepare our camp.

Fortunately the spot selected was opposite to a clearing where there were several large piles of rails, ready for use. These were immediately appropriated and rigged up for a roof and floor. Meanwhile, some of the party, sent on a foraging expedition, returned with a supply of sweet potatoes and their tin cups filled with delicious honey. As we were at work, an old darkey came along in an ox-team with meal from the mill, and the poor fellow was unlucky enough to have on a rebel overcoat, the buttons of which quickly disappeared under the knives of trophy seekers. On coming to the main camp the meal was confiscated, so the old man decided that he would rather go with us to Newbern than face his master's wrath.

As night came on, the sky grew blacker and blacker, and at length the storm burst upon us in all its fury. For a time our arrangements worked nicely, and our rubber blankets formed a good protection overhead, but after a while the rain discovered the weak spots, and little streams of water began to trickle into our faces and run down our backs. Sleep was out of the question, so we all got up and huddled about the embers of the smouldering fire, but to little purpose. The heavens seemed literally to have opened their flood-gates, and the floods descended. If we stepped off the rails we immediately sank knee-deep in mud, and our beds would have delighted the soul of the most fastidious porker; drenched from head to foot, with no prospect of even a wink of sleep, we waited as patiently as might be for the coming day.

Towards morning the storm abated in violence; so we built up a roaring fire, and made ourselves comparatively comfortable, our spirits returning with the light, and by ration time we were as bright as if we had passed a most delightful night. Having dried our clothes and blankets as well as the circumstances permitted, about nine o'clock we rejoined the regiment, most of whom had been drowned out in the night, and suffered an experience similar to our own. The cavalry had returned in the night, after riding about thirty miles, their progress having been stopped by the burning of a bridge near Onslow Court House. They were followed back by a long procession of contrabands, with faces turned eastward.

About half-past nine that same morning, we started

on our return march. The rain had subsided into a fine drizzle, and the roads were somewhat inclined to be muddy. The head of the column pushed along as though hotly pursued by the enemy, stopping for about twenty minutes at the end of the first five miles. We hurried on through Pollocksville without halting, taking a breathing spell and dinner just beyond the village, and then the fun commenced. Mud was king that day. Not like our New England mud, barely deep enough to soil your boots, but real old Southern mud, fathomless, immeasurable. Every little while we were greeted with solemn farewells by unfortunate ones disappearing rapidly from view, bound on a terrestrial voyage to China by the air, or rather earth, line. One poor wretch, stepping into a deceitful puddle, descended to his waist; then, unable to proceed either up or down, concluded to remain where he was, for want of a better place, until, having furnished much sport to the crowd, two of his comrades, taking pity on his helpless condition, seized him by the shoulders, and landed him once more on *terra firma*.

Every mile or two, streams, intended for peaceful, babbling brooks, but which, swollen by the rains, had became raging torrents and angry rivers on a small scale, crossed the road. Some we forded, others we waded for lack of better means of transit. Occasionally rail bridges spanned the stream at the side of the road, tempting the unwary one, and some unlucky one would now and then disappear from them into the roaring flood, and emerge looking quite moist and crestfallen, with his gun in excellent order for use. Little streaks of clay cropped up here and there along the road, holding the feet as in a vice, and he was lucky who retained his shoes in the struggle. Still, on rushed the van, as if life itself was at stake, if camp were not reached at an early hour; so, resigning ourselves to our fate, we tumbled along with the rest. The column must have resembled in appearance the army in the stampede of Bull Run. Every man running a race with his neighbor, all discipline thrown to the winds, and the one who reached camp first, the best fellow.

Although, without exception, the hardest day in all our campaign, we never had a merrier one. There were more jokes in that afternoon than in an ordinary month; and it may be set down as an axiom, that, in the army, the harder the work, and the more dismal the circumstances, the better humor the men will be in. But all misery has an end, and so did ours; for, about five o'clock that Saturday afternoon, we found ourselves safe and sound in the old barracks, without having fired a gun or lost a man. So ended our second expedition, we having on this last day marched, in a little more than seven hours, including all halts, twenty-one miles, on the muddiest road it has ever been our lot to see, or hope to see, disfigure the face of the earth.

In addition to the letters from home, pleasing rumors greeted us on our return, to the effect, that, for a time at least, we were to know no more expeditions, but were soon to take up our quarters in Newbern as provost guard. After time to rest and discuss this good news in its every possible feature, we were rewarded for past labors by the reading of the order for the 45th Mass., Colonel Codman commanding, to relieve the 17th Mass., at Newbern, on the 25th instant.

The intervening time was spent in preparations for departure, collecting our numerous movables, taking down shelves, hiring donkey-carts, etc., and on the 24th we retired to our bunks in old Camp Amory for the last time, the anticipation of the morrow engrossing every thought, and rendering sleep of little moment.

QUARTERS OF COMPANY A, AT NEWBERN.

CHAPTER VIII.

LIFE IN NEWBERN.

AT an early hour on the long-expected day, the detail for guard left the camp, and soon after breakfast, the rest of the regiment started, in the best possible spirits, for its new quarters, making quite a triumphal entry into the captured city, with band playing and colors flying. Crossing the railroad bridge, we marched directly to Broad street, the parade-ground of all troops occupying the city. There the out-going regiment, the 17th Mass., were drawn up in line to welcome the new-comers; and after the customary manœuvres required by military etiquette, the command of the city was tendered to Colonel Codman, and the companies ordered to their respective quarters.

The lines of Company A had ever fallen in pleasant places, and our good luck did not desert us, for we found ourselves in possession of the nicest of the houses assigned to the regiment; in fact, one of the prettiest places in the town. It was a two-storied, wooden building, on Pollock street, the principal street of Newbern, lighted with gas, but of course wholly destitute of furniture. It had flower-gardens in front and on both sides, while in the rear were one or two acres of land covered with various kinds of fruit-trees, several fig-trees among the number. There was also a cook-house, barn, and out-buildings, all, except the barn, fitted up with bunks for the accommodation of those who could not obtain a corner in the main building.

All the rooms in the house, excepting those reserved for the officers, were lined with bunks, the parlor alone having seventeen occupants. The name of "Pierce" still adorned the front door, and we would embrace this opportunity to tender to the individual rejoicing in the name of "Pierce," our most sincere thanks for the noble manner in which he retired to the country and generously yielded up his house and grounds, rent free, to the use of the Yankee soldiery.

Company K occupied the next house, and opposite them were the quarters of Company D, while across the street was the house occupied by General Hill, the rebel commander, for his headquarters when in the city. Just below, on the next corner, was the building employed by the provost marshal, and the headquarters of the provost guard. The companies were somewhat scattered, for the greater security of the city.

The duty of the provost guard was somewhat as follows. The city was divided into three districts; the first district was the south-eastern part of the town, and embraced the business quarter, having its headquarters at the provost marshal's. Here was the guard-house, where all persons arrested were kept till examination was made and sentence passed over them, — like the station-house of the police. The second district comprised the northern portion of the town, having its headquarters in the old office of the Atlantic and North Carolina Railroad. This was situated next the depot, and the desk and safe of the company remained in their old places. General Foster's headquarters, and the house occupied by his family, were in this district, and under the especial care of the guard. The third district covered the remainder of the town, the south-western portion, and was the least important of the three.

The daily detail for guard was as follows: One captain, three lieutenants, three sergeants, ten corporals and one hundred and ninety-seven privates. The absence of two companies, G and I, and the large number of men on detached service, rendered the duty of the privates quite arduous, as the large detail necessitated their going on guard every other day, with an occasional interval of two days; but the officers, non-commissioned as well as commissioned, had a very easy time of it.

Guard-mounting took place on Broad street, every morning at eight o'clock, and was quite an attraction for idlers, the band always taking part. After the customary manœuvres, each lieutenant marched his guard to the district assigned him, so that it was nearly ten o'clock by the time the old guard was relieved and returned to quarters. The men at the head of the line were assigned to the first district, and as that was the most popular of the three, there was a regular race every morning for the first place, and sometimes an enterprising company would be on hand half an hour before the required time. But, after a while, the companies alternated in their position in the line, and so all competition was at an end.

The guard was divided into three reliefs; the first being on duty from nine to one, both morning and night; the second from one to five, and the third from five to nine. The first relief was through with its labor at one o'clock A. M., while the third had the whole night from nine to five to sleep, and the day to loaf, so the choice between these two was about equally divided, but the second relief, being a sort of nondescript, was scouted by all.

There were two detached stations, both under command of a corporal, which were very much liked by the men. The first was at the railroad bridge, which, as the main entrance to the city, for all on foot or horseback, was an important point. More than one poor corporal lost his stripes when at this post, for some slight dereliction of duty. There were sentry-boxes on the bridge for stormy weather, and a cosy little guard-room with a nice bed of shavings, much more comfortable than the hard boards in the other guard-rooms. No one was allowed to pass over the bridge in either direction without a permit, and special instructions were issued against allowing any vehicle to cross without an order from department headquarters.

The other station was at the Pollock Street Jail, — jail in name, but nothing but a large wooden dwelling-house. It was occupied by rebel prisoners, disloyal citizens, and occasionally by a United States officer under arrest. The jailer was a great burly corporal of the 23d Massachusetts, who was afterwards promoted to a lieutenancy in the North Carolina native regiment. The guns of the sentries here were always loaded, and the orders were to shoot on the slightest attempt to escape,— a very necessary precaution, where but two men kept guard over a house having at times as many as sixty prisoners. Their fare was the same as that furnished to our men, and often better. The prisoners brought in were for the most part a wretched-looking set of men; dirty to filthiness, ragged, ignorant and stupid, many of them the clay-eaters of North Carolina. There was a rebel surgeon confined there for a long time, an intelligent, educated man from New Orleans, with whom we had many a talk on the topics of the day, upon which he kept himself well informed.

There was a great choice in the sentry-stations over the city, and the men very quickly became acquainted with their various excellences and respective merits. Some were under cover, others were not needed at night; at this one a breakfast was furnished by a kind neighbor, at another, the guard was sure of some dinner, while some were wholly undesirable, being on some bleak, unprotected corner, exposed to wind and rain.

Guard duty had sufficient variety to relieve it from monotony, and while many a ludicrous scene happened, occasionally, occurrences not wholly devoid of danger, served to keep us alive. Some one would report a disturbance, and ask for a guard to restore peace; whereupon volunteers would be called for, and two or three start off, ready for anything that might turn up. Some drunken soldier has, perhaps, made himself at home in a house, to the obvious discomfort of the inmates, and refuses to be dislodged; but the ugly look of the bayonet soon brings him to terms, and he is marched off to the guard-house, and allowed an opportunity to consider his evil ways, in solitary confinement. Occasionally, one with enough liquor to make him ugly, refuses to show his pass, and even attempts to seize the gun of the guard, when most unexpectedly, he receives the butt of the musket in his face, and, beginning to realize that "discretion is the better part of valor," submits, and is led off, a soberer and wiser man.

When some of the old New York and Pennsylvania regiments were encamped near the town, their men were very apt to make trouble during their visits to Newbern, and it often ended in their passing the night at the guard-house. One afternoon, two six-foot Irishmen came over the bridge, and on entering the town, refused to show their passes. Both had guns and bayonets, and threatened to kill any one who should attempt to arrest them. It was not until aid arrived from the guard-house, and they had been stretched out with the butt of a pistol, that they quieted down and consented to go and be locked up. Once we were stopped in the street by a native, and asked to come and arrest a drunken fellow, who had threatened to stab his wife, the niece of my informant. Although unaccustomed to interfere in family troubles, such a summons could not be neglected. The man was a citizen of Newbern, and on our arrival was asleep on a sofa, while the poor wife was weeping in the cook-house. Arousing him, we made known our errand; and the accusations and tears of the wife, together with the maudlin stupidity of the man, were pitiful to witness. It is to be hoped that three day's solitary confinement, on bread and water, brought him to a realizing sense of his conjugal duties.

One day, a person just arrived from Fortress Monroe, made complaint at the provost marshal's, of the theft of some of his baggage by one of the hands employed on the steamer. A guard was immediately sent to the steamer to arrest the criminal, and a portion of the stolen goods was found among the effects of one of the firemen, but the man himself was missing. Feeling convinced however, that the fellow was concealed somewhere on the vessel, they commenced a search, high and low, for the guilty one, and just as they were about to give up in despair, one of the guard chanced to look under one of the boilers, and there discovered the culprit, squeezed in almost out of sight. On being requested to come forth, he refused flatly, and being out of reach he could not be dragged out. A loaded pistol was produced, and aimed at his head, when some one suggested the hose, and a stream of dirty water was quickly brought to bear on the hapless victim. In vain did he squirm and writhe; he had to succumb, and finally crawled out from his hiding-place more dead than alive, and was carried in triumph to the guard-house to answer for his sins.

We were by no means idle on the days off guard. Four times a week, when the weather permitted,—and the days were rare when it did not permit,— we were indulged in the delights of brigade drill. Coming off guard at ten o'clock, the order would sound through the yard, immediately after dinner, which was earlier on those days, "Fall in for brigade drill, blouses and caps!" and at noon we formed regimental line on Broad street, and from there marched a long two miles over the railroad bridge, to the plain near our old barracks on the Trent. Here we were joined by the 17th,

43d and 51st Mass., and manœuvred by Colonel Amory for two or three hours. "Echelon by battalion at forty paces," "form line of battle on third battalion, right in front," etc., became as familiar as household words, and all of us felt competent to handle a brigade. Still it was always a happy moment when we saw our commander sheathe his long sabre, and no order was obeyed with such celerity and precision, as the one which invariably followed this action, "march off your battalions." The men were always in the best of spirits on the march back to town, and many a song and joke beguiled the weary way.

Twice a week, also, we had battalion drill, sometimes in the streets, and occasionally in one of the fields on the outskirts of the town. As we were very apt to have spectators during our street drills, the colonel was especially vexed at any blunders committed by the officers, and woe betide the unfortunate one who incurred his censure on those days, for he spoke his mind on the spot, to the great delight of the file, and the discomfiture of the rank.

But all this drill was not thrown away, and for accuracy and quickness of movements, we yielded the palm to no regiment in the department. The great feature of the day, however, was the dress-parade. Every afternoon, a little before five o'clock, there was a general struggle for blacking and brushes, "dress coats and hats" being the countersign for the hour. Nightly, with our white gloves and good clothes, we formed company in the back yard, where we had a preliminary drill in the manual, to get our hand in for the show performance. Then off we marched to the parade-ground on the next street, occasionally going through with a battalion drill, on our own account, while on the way to our place in line.

The regiment stretches along the north side of the street and the colonel takes his station on the opposite sidewalk, which is regularly occupied by a long row of lookers-on. Here, as elsewhere, our company was in good luck, having the centre of the line, and as the best drilling was to be seen there, it was accordingly directly opposite the fair faces, who deigned to grace our parade with their presence. Many thanks, fair ladies, for the innocent pleasure your bright faces afforded us poor fellows, many of whom, for eight weary months, did not so much as speak to a lady. Nor was your presence simply a pleasure but a benefit to the regiment; for what man could look aught but neat and tidy with such eyes to criticise? who would not excel in drill to win applause from such lips?

When, occasionally, the familiar face of some Boston gentleman appeared in the crowd, it was pleasant to see the start of amazement with which he greeted the first strains of music as the band beat down the line. Could these be the same men who labored so hard at Readville to produce some semblance to music? The band had indeed improved wonderfully, and it was now a positive pleasure to hear them play. Guard-mounting and dress-parade, from being a decided bore, had come to be really enjoyable. Nothing is more enlivening and inspiriting than good martial music; it relieves the monotony of all military parades, and refreshes the weary both in body and soul. When one is exhausted with marching, and to drag one leg after the other is a sore task, let the band strike up, and the inspiring sounds infuse new life into the tired frame; it makes the way look short and easy, which, but the moment before, had seemed interminable. Nor were the duties of the band confined to the department of music; for on the field of battle they did excellent work as members of the ambulance corps, and all who had need of their assistance will remember with unceasing gratitude their kind service and tender care.

REAR VIEW OF QUARTERS OF COMPANY A.

CHAPTER IX.

THE GRAND REVIEW.

IT was our good fortune during our stay in Newbern, to participate in a grand review of the 18th Army Corps by our commander, General Foster. We had due notice, and were gotten up in a state of blackness and brightness well nigh bordering on perfection. Blackness having reference to the state of our boots and equipments, brightness to our guns and brasses. The cleansing and polishing and furbishing one does in the army is beyond belief, for by the time you have come to the end of the long list of articles which require touching up, the first strap or brass, as the case may be, has become dull, and you begin again;—but to return to the review.

The day was all that could be desired, bright and beautiful, and as the regiment formed line on the parade-ground, looking so neat and nice, with colors flying, and the band outdoing itself in the excitement of the day, we felt proud of our State and the service which enlisted such men in its ranks.

The review was on the south side of the Trent, the country there affording splendid facilities for military manœuvres on a large scale, as it presented an unbroken stretch of nearly two miles in each direction. We were well acquainted with the spot, having trodden almost every foot of land thereabouts in our numerous brigade drills, and were first on the ground that day, as befitted our position in line, the Forty-fifth ranking as 1st Battalion, 1st Brigade, 1st Division, 18th Army Corps.

It was a beautiful sight to watch the long line of troops which filed over the bridge, their bayonets flashing in the sunlight, as regiment after regiment came up and took its place in line. The line was formed in brigades, four regiments deep, in the order of the brigades, our brigade holding the right, the artillery and cavalry occupying the extreme left.

The thunder of the artillery announced the arrival of our gallant commander, Major-General Foster, and soon he appeared at our front, finely mounted, and attended by his full staff. Drums are ruffled and arms presented, while the band plays "Hail to the Chief," as he dashes along in his inspection of each regiment, the music continuing while he is passing through the brigade, then the next band takes up the strain.

After a long rest and a lunch by all who had been prudent enough to bring a supply of hard-tack in their pockets, our turn came for an active part in the proceedings of the day. General Foster had taken his station on a slight eminence, and sat facing the centre of the line, which, brigade deep, extended for full a mile. Surrounded by his staff, he was the object of attraction of the crowd of spectators who thronged about him, from Mrs. Foster and her brilliant staff of ladies, down to the most ragged contraband in all that motley assembly.

As we wheeled by platoons and marched in review, the sight which greeted us was one long to be remembered for its grandeur and beauty. Line upon line of unbroken ranks stretched on as far as the eye could reach. Over each regiment waved our beautiful flag, its colors glowing with unwonted richness in the warm winter's sun, the bayonets throwing back flashes of light, and the artillery and cavalry relieving the scene from all monotony, while the Neuse, sparkling in the sunlight, and its distant bank covered with the forest evergreen, formed a perfect background for this gorgeous picture. Then there was the long row of spectators, some, seated in vehicles of all sorts and descriptions, others, mounted on animals ranging from the finest charger to the scrubbiest donkey, while on foot was a crowd composed of every age, sex and color. In their midst sat our commander, patiently awaiting our approach.

As we drew near, the band filed off to the left, and took its position directly opposite the general, where it continued playing till our brigade had all passed, when it was relieved by the next band, and once more took its place in line. As each platoon passed, the general saluted, while he honored the colors by removing his hat, the band also giving the customary salute. Battalion after battalion, battery after battery, troop after troop, they came, till the first battalion, making the complete circuit, came upon the rear of the last troop, thus forming an unbroken circle. As each regiment reached the place of starting, it halted until the long, glittering array was once more in position, then again the artillery thundered forth the salute, and the grand review was over.

Not long after this we were gladdened by the arrival of a party of ladies and gentlemen, friends of the regiment, and those amongst us who were not personally acquainted with any of the visitors, were, notwithstanding, pleased to see the familiar faces, and witness the joy of those who were made happy in their coming. We were favored on the next Sunday by a sermon from Dr. Lothrop, of Boston, who was one of the party, and it seemed strange indeed to listen to him there, preaching in a southern pulpit to an audience of soldiers. The Presbyterian church was the one occupied by us, and our chaplain held service there every Sunday afternoon, the regiment and visitors filling the body of the house. It was a plain, old-fashioned building, with a high pulpit and small organ.

The Episcopal church was open in the morning, Major Sturgis, in the absence of the rector, reading the service and a sermon. The singing by a quartette of male voices, two from our regiment, and two on detailed service in the city, would have shamed most northern choirs. The church was built of stone, and was very prettily situated on Pollock street, standing back from the street, in an old burying-ground filled with elms and willows and moss-covered tombstones. The interior of the building was finished in very good taste, and there was a fair organ, which we often went up into the organ-loft to listen to, as one of the musicians of our company had access to the building. A Sunday school was also started during our stay in town, and was very successful, increasing rapidly in size and influence.

But the most remarkable service it was our lot ever to witness, was one held in the contraband Methodist church. A small party of us, having obtained passes started one Sunday for the church in the Second District, and on entering the building, found the galleries were reserved for visitors and already well filled with soldiers, drawn there, like ourselves, by curiosity. The body of the house was crowded with the congregation of worshippers, the women occupying one side of the church, the men the other. Every shade of color from that of Erebus, god of night, to fair-haired Aurora, child of the morning, was there represented, while the bright colors which adorned the female portion of the house, added to the brilliancy of the scene.

The pulpit was unoccupied, but the leader of the meeting, an intelligent looking man, nearly white, and with, what was remarkable, sandy hair, sat in a chair in front of the pulpit. He opened the service with singing, reading a line from the hymn, which was then sung by the congregation; then reading the second line, and so on. Having heard so much of the melody of the negro, and the beautiful singing to be heard on the plantations, our expectations were highly raised, but, alas! no sooner had the first note reached our ears, than our hopes were dashed to the ground. Imagine some old psalm tune, screamed forth, line by line, from the cracked throats of the old, and by the shrill voices of the young, all singing the air, each voice pitched on a different key, and some idea of their style of music may be formed.

Next came a prayer, in which the voice of the leader was for the most part drowned in the vigorous groans of the congregation, except when it rose to a shout and was heard above the din around him. The audience having warmed to the subject, he began to exhort them to repentance. Meantime, two or three women throwing their bonnets and shawls on the pulpit stairs, evidently preparing for work, began with as many men, pillars of the church, to move about among the congregation, addressing a word here and there to enforce the preacher's remarks.

Several soon began to feel the arrow of conviction, and were led up in front of the pulpit, where the girls were stripped of shawls and bonnets, which were thrown in a heap on the stairs. The cause of this strange proceeding soon became apparent, for the poor creatures, excited and wrought into a state of frenzy by the words of the speakers, began to scream and shriek, struggling with those who were exhorting them, shouting, "Save me now," at the top of their lungs, until they fairly went into convulsions.

One poor girl, not more than sixteen or seventeen years old, struggled and screamed for more than an hour in a most frightful manner, until at length she sank on the floor utterly exhausted by her violence. It was the same on the men's side, though they were less violent in their emotions, but when the excitement was at its height, it seemed as though Bedlam itself was let loose. The scene was at once ludicrous and saddening. It was sad to think these poor creatures could hope to win salvation in such a manner, yet at the same time, the absurdity and comicality of the whole affair was irresistible, and showed a phase of negro character both strange and amusing.

As the season advanced, the weather became most delightful. The buds began to swell and the flowers to peep up here and there, until we soon found ourselves living in a great garden. Almost every house had some land about it, and our own quarters were surrounded by rose trees, violets and other plants too numerous to mention. The air teemed with fragrance from the blossoms of the apple, peach and pear trees which grew back of the house; little green figs began to make their appearance, and the elms which filled the streets once more donned their summer covering, while our ears were delighted with the song of the mocking-birds and most of our northern songsters.

Every letter sent northwards was freighted with a little offering of flowers, whose sweetness still lingered about the paper even after their freshness had passed away, and gave to friends at home some token of that summer we were enjoying, but which to them was still far distant. Pitching quoits, or rather horse-shoes, was the great amusement of the day, and engrossed the leisure hours alike of officers and men. Base ball also had its share of attention, and a small set of gymnastic apparatus was set up in the yard. Some of us, occasionally, passed a morning hour in teaching; for shortly after the arrival of the chaplain's wife, a day school was opened under her auspices for the contrabands. It was more especially intended for children, but was open to all of a more advanced age, who were anxious to learn.

The school was held daily for an hour in the colored church on Hancock street, the teachers being for the most part, men of our regiment, assisted by two or three ladies, who interested themselves in the work. The scholars were, as a rule, quite bright and very eager to learn, and seemed much delighted with their primers and spelling-books. Their progress in reading was quite rapid, their eagerness to acquire the knowledge from which they had been hitherto barred, overcoming all obstacles. The young ones were sometimes seen going over their lessons at home for the edification of the older ones, who were unable to attend the school, thus bringing a double blessing on the labors of the teacher. After we left Newbern and once more went into camp, the chaplain opened a school there for the benefit of the contraband settlement near by, which was kept up till our departure, and was not without good results.

The receipt of frequent mails and occasional boxes from home, served as pleasant little episodes, oases in the desert of our life of drill and guard. The joy which beamed on the countenances of those who read their names in staring letters on the boxes found piled up in the yard, on returning from drill, was amusing to behold, and showed that the appetite for home cookery was not wholly destroyed by long neglect.

The mail steamers made known their approach by blowing three whistles when some distance down the river, and, no sooner was the signal heard, than cries of "Dudley Buck!" "Ellen Terry!" "Mail! Mail!" would resound through the quarters, and some of the more enterprising ones would travel down to the wharf to count the number of mail bags, for our expectations were gauged by the number of bags. After two or three hours of impatient waiting, the orderly would go over to the regimental post-office, which was under the charge of the chaplain, and quickly return loaded down with the precious freight.

Then the answers must be written immediately, for the mail boats made but little stay, and the notice on the post-office announcing the hour of mail closing, is frequently consulted, for it had a way of changing from hour to hour, which was apt to be embarrassing. Permission to keep the lights burning after taps is obtained, and the table in those rooms that boast such a luxury, is surrounded by busy writers. The more prudent ones, who have already mailed their letters, turn into their bunks in the vain hope of profiting by their forethought by getting an extra amount of sleep, but the light and noise prove too much for them, and they amuse and revenge themselves by annoying and worrying the writers. The result is, that a riot, in a small way, is pretty sure to follow, which ends in the appearance of the captain, and the extinction of the lights, when the prudent ones once more turn in, chuckling over their triumph. Their rejoicing, however, is ill-timed, for the others, baffled in their attempts to write, determine that no one shall sleep till they see fit, and by noise and talk keep their poor victims on the rack, till, wearied out at last, silence at last reigns over the scene of confusion, and sweet sleep and dreams of home descend.

CHAPTER X.

THE FOURTEENTH OF MARCH.

IT was General Foster's intention to celebrate the anniversary of the battle of Newbern, and the capture of the town, by a parade of the troops in and about the city, and orders to that effect had been issued to the different commanders. But a slight circumstance occurred on the day previous to the anniversary, which caused an entire change in the programme.

We had often heard from prisoners the boast that Newbern should not remain in our possession for more than a year, and, sure enough, on the 13th, the pickets were driven in, and, instead of a parade, there seemed to be every prospect of a fight. All were actively engaged in preparation for whatever the morrow might bring forth. Aides and orderlies were galloping through the streets, and ammunition wagons carrying supplies to the various forts, while the natives hung about the corners with ill-suppressed looks of exultation on their yellow faces, eagerly listening to the scraps of news which the passing soldiers let fall. Cartridges were given out, and the guns of the guard, contrary to custom, were loaded, and strict orders given to arrest any who breathed even the faintest suspicion of treason.

After a restless night, we were aroused early on the morning of the 14th by the booming of cannon and bursting of shells, and quickly started out to learn the immediate condition of affairs. The eastern bank of the Neuse, for some miles above and below the town, is covered with an impenetrable swamp. There is, however, one approach by a road from Little Washington, which strikes the river about a mile above the upper end of the town, and, in old times, a ferry-boat plied the river at this point. This ferry had fallen into disuse, as our communications with Washington were wholly by water, but the importance of securing this approach, and preventing any surprise in that direction, had not been overlooked, and, for some time past, there had been a picket-station across the river. This was now occupied by the 92d New York, who had been busily engaged in throwing up a strong earthwork, commanding the road, but as yet no guns had been mounted.

We soon discovered that this camp was the point of attack, and nothing but the cowardice of the enemy, and the bravery of the 92d, saved the latter from capture or destruction. At an early hour, their pickets had been driven in, and soon after daybreak the enemy appeared, about an eighth of a mile from the earthwork, with a force of some five thousand infantry and cavalry, and sixteen pieces of artillery. Imagine the situation; between three and four hundred men armed only with muskets, confronted by a force of more than ten to one. Protected, it is true, by earthworks, but without a gun mounted, while behind them stretched a mile and a half of water, separating them from friends and safety; and about a mile down the river, half hidden in the morning mist, lay the gunboat "Hunchback," unconscious of the threatened danger.

The rebel general sends a summons to surrender, which is met some distance from the works to prevent too close an inspection of their weakness, and is answered by the brave commander with an "If you want the place, you must come and take it." No sooner is this reply received than the ball is opened. But the first boom of the cannon is a signal of alarm to friendly ears across the river; it startles the sleepers on the gun-boat and arouses the people in the city.

Thick and fast the storm of shot and shell pours in upon the devoted little garrison. Tents are riddled, shanties knocked in pieces, but the men themselves, lying close behind their entrenchments are, as yet, unharmed. Can they hold out till rescue comes, or will the enemy carry the works by storm? is the anxious thought of every heart, as with straining eyes they watch the signs of life now discernable on the gun-boat, on which their hopes depend. At last the smoke curls up from the tall pipe and the old "Hunchback" moves slowly to the rescue. Like the passing vessel, which has seen the signal of the shipwrecked mariner and is gradually lessening the distance between him and a watery grave, so the gun-boat, steaming up the river, comes between the little garrison and captivity in a southern prison. As she neared the scene of action and her hundred pounder opened upon the enemy, their hopes of success were gone forever.

Mounted in the rigging of a schooner lying at the

provost-marshal's wharf, glass in hand, we watched the combatants. Our flag floated proudly over the works, and the smoke of the rebel guns was quickly followed by the explosion of the shells, now over the camp, now in the river, one or two even striking upon our side of the Neuse. A revenue schooner, also, was beating up the river, anxious to join in the fight, but the hundred pounder of the "Hunchback" proved too much for the visitors. With one gun dismounted by a shot from the gun-boat, and a loss of several killed and wounded, they retired discomfited into the woods, whence they sent an occasional shot at the prize which had been so unceremoniously snatched from their very grasp. The revenue vessel, of lighter draft than the gun-boat, ran in close to shore and anchored off the brave garrison, and all danger in that quarter was at an end.

Simultaneous attacks were also made on the outposts at Deep Gully and Batchelder's Creek, but were attended with no better success; so, baffled at all points, the foe gave up the attempt and retired in the direction of Kinston and Little Washington. In honor of our victory, and out of compliment to the enemy, General Foster had the Stars and Stripes hoisted to the very summit of the Episcopal steeple, the highest point in the city, where, visible for miles in every direction, they floated in proud defiance over the place in which one year before had drooped the tricolor of treason and rebellion.

The hope and exultation so visible that morning in the faces of the traitorous inhabitants, gradually paled into a yellower despair than ever, and the stores of provisions prepared by them in anticipation of the speedy coming of their friends, ferreted from their concealment by the vigilance of the detectives, met with an untimely end. The town soon recovered from the excitement caused by this near approach of the enemy, and we all enjoyed the occurrences of the day as a pleasant variety in our rather monotonous life.

But, while we were enjoying a life of comparative comfort in Newbern, with unlimited credit at the sutler's, relying on the arrival of the paymaster some time in the future, other regiments in the department were less fortunate. The siege of Little Washington by the rebels began, and we listened daily to the distant booming of cannon. But though regiment after regiment was sent off, until only three or four were left about the city, and the rest of our brigade participated in General Spinola's fruitless attempt to march overland to Washington, raise the siege, and rescue General Foster from his uncomfortable, not to say dangerous, situation, our regiment continued in its old routine of guard duty, having besides special charge of the city defences in the absence of the other troops.

At last, on the night of April 16, General Foster ran the blockade in the little steamer "Escort," not without great danger to himself and the crew, for they passed through a very hot fire, and the steamer was struck in several places. The pilot was killed, and one shot went through the coppers in the cook's galley, taking off an arm of the cook in its passage; another passed through the general's state-room, fortunately unoccupied at the time. There was, of course, great risk incurred in running by the enemy's batteries, for any injury to the machinery would have insured capture or destruction, but the urgent need for General Foster's presence in Newbern caused all personal danger to be regarded as nothing in the service of the country. No time was lost upon his arrival, and that very day troops were on the way, some by land, others by water, to the relief of the beleaguered town, and before a week passed, the siege was raised and the enemy had disappeared.

During the troubles above mentioned, a change was made in our system of guard duty, and instead of having sentry posts scattered about the town, squads of men patrolled the streets four hours at a time. This change was a great relief to the regiment, for thereby the number of men required for daily duty was reduced nearly two-thirds, and instead of going on guard every other day as before, the turns now came but once in four or five days. We got to know the town pretty well in this way, for the patrol visited every street, lane and alley in its wanderings by night as well as day, and many curious scenes and places met our eyes, which in ordinary life would never have been visible.

But pleasant things must have an end. Rumors became prevalent through the regiment that we were soon to be relieved, and the honorable duty of provost guard to be assigned to the 44th Mass., as a reward for their services at Little Washington. The following order, read on dress-parade, confirmed our fears:

HEADQUARTERS DEPARTMENT OF NORTH CAROLINA,
18TH ARMY CORPS,
NEWBERN, April 23, 1863.

SPECIAL ORDER NO. 117, NO. 5.

In accordance with the custom of the Department, the regiment now doing provost duty will be relieved. The commanding general, on changing the guard of the town, desires to convey to Colonel Codman, and through him, to his officers and men, his high appreciation of the manner in which the duties of the guard have been performed.

He has noticed with great pleasure the drill, discipline and general efficiency of the regiment. The 44th Regiment, M. V. M., will relieve the 45th on Saturday, the 25th inst., at 9.00 A. M.

By command of Major-General Foster.

[Signed]   L. HOFFMAN, A. A. G.

A very pleasant testimonial of the good feeling which prevailed between the inhabitants of the town and the regiment, was also received by the colonel, which read as follows:

NEWBERN, N. C., April 25, 1863.

COLONEL C. R. CODMAN, OFFICERS AND MEN OF THE 45TH M. V. M.

Gentlemen:— Having learned with regret that your regiment is about to retire from the duty of guarding the city, I beg leave on behalf of all loyal citizens, myself, my family, and other families here, to render you our sincere thanks for the efficiency and courtesy with which you have discharged your duties.

It has seldom been our lot to see a body of soldiers so uniformly civil and gentlemanly in their behavior, temperate and orderly in their habits, comparatively free from the prevailing vice of profanity, and so prompt in restraining those who, by any violence, would attempt to disturb our streets.

Accept, gentlemen, our thanks for past kindness, and wishes for your future welfare.

W. H. DOHERTY, A. M.,
Principal of Newbern Academy.

The last two or three days of our sojourn in the town, several ludicrous scenes occurred at the provost-marshal's, in consequence of the revival of an old order in respect to the uniform of the soldiers. It had become the general custom of detailed men in the various departments, to wear different articles of an officer's uniform, everything in fact but shoulder straps, rendering it impossible for the guard to distinguish between officers and privates. An order was therefore issued to the guard to deprive such men of their superfluous ornaments, and in case they refused to give them up, to conduct them to the guard-house. So, every little while, some indignant fellow would appear at the guard-house, escorted by a sentry, and demand the meaning of such shameful treatment.

The question was commonly answered by the appropriation of the forbidden finery by the officer in command, after allowing the owner to peruse the order of the provost-marshal, when he would retire from the scene somewhat crestfallen. Two examples afforded us especial mirth, the one a commissary sergeant, the other, hospital steward of a certain Massachusetts regiment, for their rage was something laughable, and their impudence so great, that they were permitted to spend the night in the guard-house as a reward.

The morning of the 25th dawned bright and pleasant, and our numerous boxes and traps were piled up in the yard, preparatory to being toted off in the funny little mule-carts. Our quarters were all swept and garnished, some of the rooms having been trimmed with flowers in honor of the new comers. We took our last breakfast at the Boston Lunch, and the first relief of the new guard having been duly posted, we bade farewell to the house which had sheltered us so comfortably and pleasantly the past three months, and joined the regimental line on Broad street, the scene of so many guard-mountings, drills and dress-parades, and now of the ceremony of tendering the command of the city to our successors. Having conformed to the requirements of military etiquette, we started for our new home in the country, Camp Massachusetts, on the banks of the Neuse.

Camp at Core Creek.

Up the Rail Road —

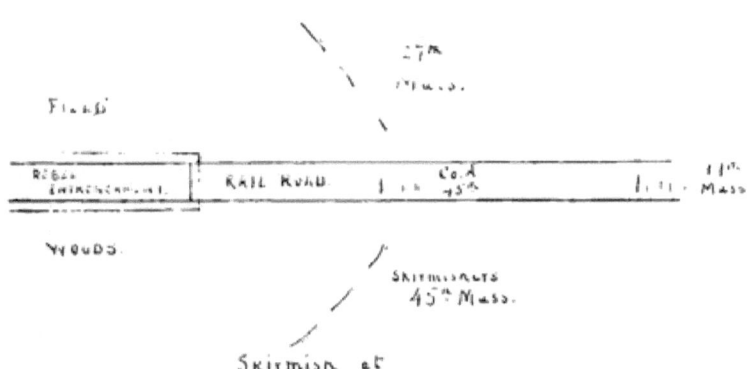

Skirmish at
Dover Cross Roads
April 28. 1863.

CHAPTER XI.

A TRIP UP THE RAILROAD.

THE evening of our second day in camp, Sunday, April 26, we received an unexpected favor from General Foster, in the shape of an order to march the next morning. The regiment was quickly astir, for rations were to be made ready, cartridge-boxes filled, and all those little preparations gone through with which marching orders always render necessary. After a while, quiet settles down, and we turn in, determined to make sure of one more good sleep at all events. We are roused at early dawn by the roll of the drum; the roll is called, the "Blind Girl" manages to fire off his rifle, fortunately without injury to the bystanders, the regimental line is formed, and we start for Newbern.

On arriving in town, it appears that the expedition consists of the first division of infantry, accompanied by a small force of cavalry and artillery, the destination being somewhere in the direction of Kinston. The Forty-Fifth meets with its usual good luck, for our brigade is embarked on the cars, with orders to proceed by rail as far as the track will allow, thereby saving us a march of some eighteen miles, which the other brigade is compelled to make. The whole force was under the command of General Palmer.

After the usual delay in getting men and horses on board the cars, we moved slowly up the road, which, passing through the camps and entrenchments surrounding the town on this side, runs for miles in an almost straight line through the pine forest, broken here and there by a clearing, and an occasional picket or signal station. After a ride of some twelve miles we reached the outpost at Batchelder's Creek, then held by the 58th Penn., Colonel Jones. Their camp was surrounded by earthworks, and a strong blockhouse commanded the railroad and bridge across the creek, where a row of sharpened stakes presented an ugly front to any hostile visitor.

The centre of attraction was, however, a railroad monitor, which stood on a side-track. It was an iron-plated baggage-car, with a peaked roof, the skylight serving for an entrance, which was reached by a ladder on the outside, removable in time of need. It carried two rifled six-pounders, one at each end, for which there were port-holes in the sides and ends of the car, thus giving the gunners range both of the railroad and surrounding country. The sides of the car were covered with rifles, and pierced with loop-holes for their use, the whole affair being surmounted by the old flag. This formidable arm of the service accompanied us to our camping-ground, where it remained during our sojourn.

About six miles beyond Batchelder's Creek, we were dumped from the platform cars, much after the manner of dumping gravel, into an open field bordering on a small stream, boasting the name of Gore Creek. The clearing extended on both sides of the railroad, the farmer's house and barn forming the prominent feature in the scene. These were immediately placed under guard to prevent any depredation by unlawful hands.

The family had not left the house, perhaps having been wholly overcome by the unexpectedness of our visit. The poor man had most unfortunately planted his corn and grain, and there is great reason to fear that a love for the Union did not prevail in his mind when he beheld his crop trampled under the feet of Union soldiers, and his nice rail fences vanish in the smoke of their fires. No unnecessary damage was inflicted, but when three or four regiments are encamped for several days on a planted field, you cannot expect very much of a harvest.

As the whole afternoon was before us, we at once set to work to make our bivouac more than ordinarily comfortable. Rails being the first requisite, we collected quite a pile, and then commenced on our shanty. Planting two rails firmly in the ground, inclined towards each other and crossing a little at the top in this manner X, we secured them in this position with blanket straps, and the length of a rail distant, planted two more in like manner. A rail laid in the notches formed the ridge-pole of our house, and rails slanted from this pole to the ground completed the frame-work. The covering for the roof consisted of our rubber blankets, making a waterproof hut, of which we were very thankful before our stay in that spot was over.

Our next care after completing the hut, was to procure a good bed, which we soon accomplished by felling two or three pines and lopping off the small branches, these making a delightfully soft and springy mattress. After a very comfortable night's rest, we amused ourselves in exploring the brook which ran through a pleasant little vale close by the camp, and idled about till noon. While wondering whether it was not time for dinner, the drums began to sound the "assembly," followed immediately by the summons to "Fall in."

Colonel Amory having been compelled by sickness to return to Newbern, the command devolved upon Colonel Codman. Accompanied by a portion of the 17th Mass., under Lieut.-Col. Fellows, we were soon on our way up the railroad, preceded by two companies of the 45th, under command of the major, as a scouting party. A short distance beyond the creek, we passed a small earth-work, where some months before a body of rebels had been surrounded and captured, and the *debris* of their camp still lay scattered about.

The track had been partially relaid for some distance, rendering the marching anything but pleasant, as there was no path on the side of the track, owing to the slippery, muddy condition of the steep banks. Moreover, the weather was extremely warm, adding much to the discomfort of the march, especially to such as had been foolish enough to wear their overcoats. Most of the men had eaten no dinner, and but one or two of the wise ones had thought to bring anything with them.

A mile or more from camp, we passed the bivouac of the two companies who had been on picket duty the previous night, and were now scouting in advance of us. As we pushed forward, all the roads which crossed the track were eagerly scanned for traces of the enemy or the column co-operating with us on the Neuse road. But nothing was to be seen until, after marching about six miles, we came upon the major, who was awaiting our approach with his little battalion at one of these cross-roads. He had discovered a body of troops on the river-road, which was quickly pronounced to be the other brigade.

The two companies which had been employed thus far in the fatiguing duty of skirmishing through the swampy country where the road ran, were left here under command of the major, as a reserve, and we hurried forward. The track had been wholly demolished from this point as far on as we went. In some places they had turned the whole body of the track, rails and sleepers, into the ditch, while in others they had burnt the sleepers, bending the rails in the fires. We found this destruction of the track rather a benefit than otherwise, for it gave us a smooth, level road, free from obstructions, and much less wearisome to march upon than where we were obliged to jump from sleeper to sleeper.

As our skirmishers advanced, they drew the fire of the enemy's pickets, who were ensconced behind little breastworks made of sleepers. The rebels fell back quickly as we came near, firing an occasional shot to spread the alarm, which was replied to on our side, but the distance was too great either to inflict or receive damage. The latter part of the afternoon, after some ten miles marching, we arrived at a large clearing extending on both sides of the track. A house and barn stood on a cross-road on the left, and the Neuse road, separated by a single field from the railroad, was on the right, and, as we subsequently discovered, crossed the track a short distance beyond. Here a halt was ordered, as, not four hundred yards distant, an earth-work loomed up directly across the track. It extended also for some distance to the left into the woods, and was concealed by a sunken fence and underbrush; the works also ran along the track to guard against an attack from the Neuse road. A squad of men sent to the house to make investigation, soon returned with two prisoners, a man and a boy, whom they had discovered making their escape from the back of the house, and after a sharp chase had captured and brought to the colonel. The old man was so frightened at having fallen into the hands of the Yankees, that very little was to be got from him. He amused us by his answer when asked his age; he said he did not know, for his house took fire once, and his age was burnt up.

Unable to ascertain the strength of the enemy, except that there was a "right smart heap," and uncertain whether they had artillery or not, the colonel decided, nevertheless, to advance without awaiting the arrival of the other column. Accordingly, five companies of the 45th filed off to the left, and deploying as skirmishers, advanced through the field back of the house, leaving the sixth company, Co. A, to guard the colors, the 17th Mass. acting as reserve. The firing soon became very brisk along the line of the works, and the enemy's force was estimated at from three to five hundred.

They did not, however, show themselves, and their firing was so high that we concluded they must have held their guns above their heads and fired at random, in their fear of exposing themselves to northern bullets. The colonel was in doubt as to the best course to pursue, for we had no artillery and he feared the rebels might have a masked battery. But as we advanced nearer and nearer, without drawing anything but musketry fire, it was deemed best to carry the works by assault, without waiting for the artillery which was with the other brigade. The order was given to Lieut.-Col. Fellows, of the 17th, to advance with his men and charge the works; but the captain of Co. A did not like to have this honor taken out of his hands, for we were in the advance; so, after some talk, the task was delegated to him. Fixing bayonets, and firing by platoons, we started on the run directly up the track.

The works were two or three hundred yards distant, and had the enemy possessed any artillery, our little company would have suffered most disastrously. But fortunately for us they had none, and at our advance gave way and fled into the woods, greeting us with a final volley as we leaped the ditch and took possession of the entrenchments, where, in their haste, they had left three of their comrades killed by our bullets. The sight of those poor fellows, lying there so still and motionless, made an indelible impression on the mind. It gave us a new insight into the character of the men we were contending with. There they lay, dressed in miserable clothing, their haggard faces, long tangled hair, and neglected beards giving them a wild, hardly human appearance.

The head of the other column arrived just as our victory was assured, but it was not thought best to penetrate any farther on account of our nearness to Kinston, only six miles distant, and not even to hold what we had gained. So, with a loss of one killed and three or four wounded, we started on the return march for camp, ten miles away. Night soon fell, and, to increase the pleasure of the way, it began to rain, gently at first, but soon with a vigor which was, under the circumstances, anything but agreeable.

Our situation was not an enviable one. In the enemy's country, not knowing but they might return at any moment with overpowering numbers; between us and camp a ten-mile's march on a partially demolished track, through thick darkness and a pelting rain. Remembering, however, that "what can't be cured must be endured," we trudged bravely on through the black night, regardless of rank or file, stumbling over the remains of the track, and only anxious to end our trials as soon as possible by a vigorous use of our legs.

Most of us had eaten nothing since morning, and one or two fairly fainted from hunger and exhaustion. Having pretty good legs of our own, we arrived at camp about nine o'clock, among the first, drenched to the skin and too tired to eat or sleep. Other poor fellows were not so fortunate, but came straggling in, in groups of two and three all through the night, some not getting in till the next morning. The march told very severely on some of the field officers who had been unable to take their horses, and were unused to such exercise; and we always felt that the colonel was more lenient to the men after that practical experience of a march.

We remained quietly in camp the next day, though the pioneers were at work on the railroad, apparently engaged in its reconstruction. But only apparently, for the object of our expedition was to retain any force the enemy might have at Kinston in that vicinity, and prevent them from giving assistance to the troops then threatening General Dix at Suffolk. A portion of the 43d Mass. went up the railroad for some distance to keep up the deception, returning the same night.

We were most agreeably surprised here by the receipt of a mail from home, which was brought up to us, and by its help we managed to pass the day very comfortably. After two very rainy nights, we were once more packed on the platform cars and landed directly at Camp Massachusetts, which lay close to the railroad, where we quickly settled down to a life of drill and stockading.

— Camp Massachusetts —

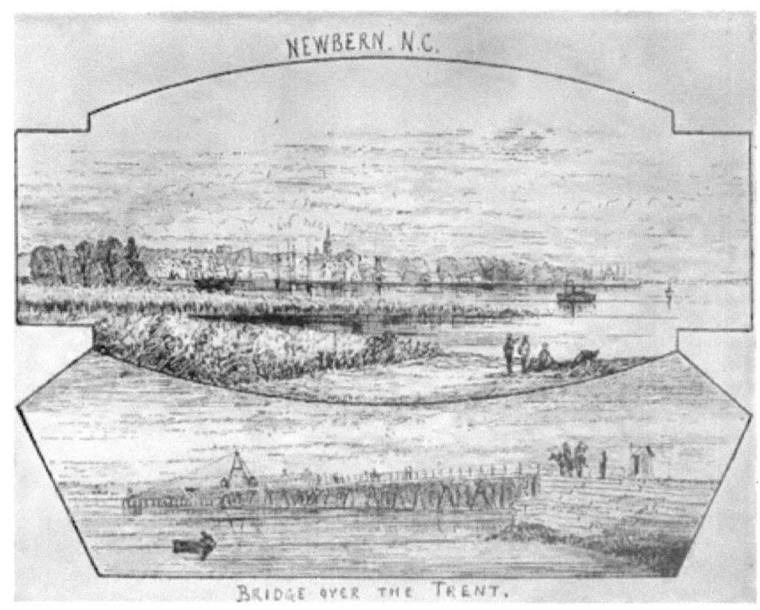

CHAPTER XII.

CAMP MASSACHUSETTS.

OUR camp, which we left so unceremoniously to go to Gum Swamp, was situated on a large plantation, about a mile and a half south of Newbern, and an eighth of a mile from the Neuse. It was but a few rods from the railroad and just outside a long line of earthworks which we were to man in case of an attack from this quarter, they being the outer line of works in this direction.

We found that the pioneers had been at work during our absence, and the camp was already laid out in streets, and some of the tents pitched. They were A tents, eight feet square, and intended for four occupants, though owing to the liberal supply many had but three; however, no one was ever heard to complain of a superabundance of room. Sunday was anything but a day of rest, for, immediately after service, there was a general stampede for the deserted camps near by, to obtain flooring for the tents and materials for stockading them.

These stockades were walls about three feet in height, eight feet square, making a foundation for the tent, and largely increasing the room and convenience. They were built in every variety of style, some of logs, after the fashion of log-houses, others with rough clap-boards, pieces of boxes, in fact anything that would answer the purpose of a board, an extremely scarce article about camp. When the work was completed the streets presented a very motley appearance, no two being alike, the looks of each stockade varying according to the skill of the builder.

The hours of grief which this herculean task of stockading entailed upon the three unfortunates sheltered by our canvass, will not soon be forgotten. Our first sorrow was, finding on our return from up country, that our upright posts, the corner stones of our foundation, selected with the greatest care and discrimination, indeed, perfect gems in their way, and sawed off into proper lengths with much labor and a dull saw, were missing, actually gone. An undeniable judgment upon us for having found them on Sunday. This was, however, but the beginning of our sorrows. After many journeys back and forth between our tent and the old camps, sufficient materials were again collected on which to commence operations.

With careful measurement and seeming accuracy, the places for the uprights were marked and the holes dug. It is due to the soil of North Carolina to say that if there was one easy thing about stockading it was this same digging holes. It reminded us of our younger days, when the sand-heaps which lay before unfinished houses were the undisputed territory of the children of the neighborhood, and castles, caves, bridges and tunnels grew under the busy hands of the young builders. Our camp was located on a sandy plain, no doubt made expressly for digging holes, whether for posts or earthworks, it mattered not.

Having erected the posts, we next proceeded to make the walls of our house. First, the sutler had no nails, and we had to wait half a day for those. The company boasts two saws and three hatchets; you spend five minutes in going up and down the street in a vain attempt to borrow either the one or the other; they are all in use; you wait in idleness for ten minutes and try again. There is no need of wasting breath in making known your errand,—the unhappy owners of the coveted articles are visited on the average by some eight or ten applicants in as many minutes,—a look is sufficient.

At last you espy a saw lying idle, and immediately pounce on it and rush to your tent. Three sticks are sawed, and you are just getting your hand in when you are confronted by the injured man who indignantly demands his property, which you are constrained with a bad grace to deliver. The same scene is enacted with the hammer; and having spent as much time as a contractor would ask to build a house, the sides are at last completed and placed in position. The fact is undeniable,—they look very rough and unworkmanlike; however, we put the best foot forward, and the worst looking side at the back, where we flatter ourselves it will not be seen.

At length the frame is ready to receive the roof, and in an agony of doubts and fears, after some effort, we raise the tent to its place, and—find that our frame is too large for the tent, or, rather, the tent is too small for the frame; at all events, it is no go. However, by dint of pulling and twisting and sawing, we drag the refractory edges together, and with our tent-poles at an angle of forty-five degrees, and presenting a most unstable appearance, we enter our new abode in triumph. We have stockaded.

The old camp life of drill and guard was re-enacted here, with an additional task, by way of variety, entitled fatigue-duty, which was neither more nor less, than spending the day in the trenches, with a spade for a companion, an occupation on a hot summer's day the reverse of delightful. Battalion drills and company drills followed each other in quick succession, but as the one was early in the morning, and the other late in the afternoon, we had a good portion of the day to ourselves, and many were the shifts to fill up the long interval.

The customary occupation in the morning, when the weather permitted, was a swim in the Neuse. After morning drill, it was usually the way to go to guard-mounting and hear the band play. Then it was time to bathe, for we were obliged by orders to go in at ten, or thereabouts, and only once a day, but this increased the sport by bringing a good many into the water at the same time. Our road to the river lay directly past the regimental hospital, most beautifully situated in a grove of magnificent mulberry trees, as large as English elms, and so thick-leaved as to make a perfect shade tree. The hospital tent was pitched under one of them, the farm-house of the plantation being also occupied for a hospital; and near by was the quartermaster's building, while within a stone's throw stood Fort Spinola.

The fort was built directly on the river-bank, and commanded, with its black-mouthed cannon, both the river and the surrounding country for more than a mile in every direction. On our arrival at Camp

Massachusetts, the fort was garrisoned by Co. G, of our regiment, who, having practiced heavy artillery drill at Fort Macon, were summoned to its defence in the early part of April, when an attack on the city was apprehended. Soon after our advent, Co. I returned from Fort Macon and took the place of Co. G at Fort Spinola, so that, after an interval of six months, the whole regiment was once more united under one command.

Just by the fort there was a long wharf, running into deep water, for the slope of the river-bed is very gradual, and this wharf was, so to speak, the headquarters of the bathers. Here were unlimited opportunities for swimming, diving, etc., while those who preferred shallower water had the whole river-bank to wade from. One of the men actually swam across the river one day, without making known his purpose. He not only reached the opposite side, but had started on his way back when he was picked up by a boat which was sent after him. As the river is fully two miles wide at this point, it was, to say the least, quite a swim.

The quartermaster's boat lay at this wharf, for all the light stores were brought from Newbern by water, the heavier ones coming in the cars. The boat was manned by a detailed crew, exempt from all other duty, but as the officers made frequent use of the boat to go to the city at all hours of the day and night, the position was no sinecure. We poor soldiers who were blessed with occasional furloughs to visit the great centre of attraction, were sometimes honored by an humble seat in the bow, for which we were duly grateful, being thereby saved a long and dusty walk.

As the season advanced, and the summer sun grew hotter and hotter, the blackberry vines, which grew in great profusion around the camp, began to exhibit a pleasing appearance of redness, which indicated a not distant day of ripeness. Hearing certain stories about a discovery which had been made in some fields not a great way off, two or three of us started out one day, dippers in hand, and, after a diligent search, were amply rewarded for our pains by a dish of delicious wild strawberries. Not content with this luxury, the colored people near by must needs bring round, just at dinner time, some nice ice-cream, and, compelled by the force of circumstances, we had a dessert of strawberries and ice-cream. We often repeated this experiment while the little red beauties were to be found, and before they had fairly disappeared another fruit had ripened.

The blackberries had passed from the red era, and acres upon acres were covered with the long trailing vines, thickly laden with the luscious fruit. There was a continuous feast among the regiments encamped in that neighborhood while the season lasted, and during that time it was our regular amusement to spend an hour or two daily in blackberrying, — a pleasant task, for a sure reward awaited us at the termination of our labors.

A favorite place to visit was the Newbern battle-field, some three miles below our camp, and one bright May morning some four or five of us started off for the day in that direction. Instead of taking the direct road which ran close by the camp, we determined to go down the river bank. Passing through the camp of the 1st North Carolina, colored, which, some time after, did such good service at Olustee, we lingered a moment to watch them drill. After admiring their powers of imitation, and, at the same time, enjoying some most ludicrous blunders, we soon found ourselves on the borders of the river.

The nature of the country was very different from what we had been led to expect, consisting of a series of bluffs and deep valleys, similar in formation to those on the Mississippi. As we approached the main line of earthworks, we found indications of rebel fortifications on these heights; old gun-carriages, sand-bags, and all the *debris* of a deserted camp lay about in hopeless ruin. They had evidently feared we would approach by the river, and we soon came upon the remains of the blockade, consisting of sunken vessels, some of which had been raised and towed up to Newbern, thus opening the channel.

We followed a pleasant little path through the woods for some distance, catching occasional glimpses of the river through the trees, as it sparkled in the bright sunlight, and at length came out at the rebel earthworks, the scene of the battle when Newbern was won. The works extend from the west side of the railroad directly to the river's edge, where they terminate in a small fort which commands the river, and which we found filled with the ruins of camp equipage of every description abandoned by the rebels in their hurried flight.

The 8th Mass. were doing picket duty at this point, and apparently having a very easy time of it. As we had all explored the ground two or three times before, we hurried along the line of works till we struck the Newbern road, where, instead of turning back to camp, we set our faces southward, hoping to obtain a dinner at one of the houses which stand some way below the battlefield. Crossing the broad cleared space over which our troops had made their gallant charge, stopping a moment to examine the traces of rebel bullets in the trees and to marvel at the terrible havoc made by the shells among the pines, we soon reached a lane which led up to a house half hidden by the trees, where we determined to try our fortune.

The usual group of negro shanties stood on the lane, running over with little picaninnies, who gazed at us with wondering eyes. The owner of the house had gone to town to lay in a stock of provisions, but his wife gave us a cordial welcome and promised to do her best for us. We were soon summoned to what was to us a most luxurious repast; the mere fact of sitting down at a table was a pleasure, and the strangeness of our surroundings enhanced the enjoyment. Having taken our dessert in a mulberry tree, the thought of the battalion drill awaiting us at the end of our walk, hastened our departure from this quiet spot, which was a delightful contrast to the stir of camp-life, and seemingly far removed from every thought of war. The lameness of the master of the house had alone prevented him from joining the army, as most of his neighbors had done. We obtained an insight into southern life in this way, which was new and interesting, and returned to camp well pleased with our excursion.

On the 16th of May the regiment was reviewed by the division commander, General Palmer, who expressed much pleasure at the appearance of the men, and particularly admired the looks of the guns. It was the custom during the mild May evenings, for the singers to collect and give impromptu concerts, and very often the band played for an hour in the square in front of the colonel's tent, while on moonlight nights, as we lay awake in our tents, we could hear the mocking-birds in the grove by the hospital, making night melodious with their songs.

There were two picket-stations connected with the camp, one about a mile and a half down the river road, prolific with mosquitos and wood-ticks; the other, and by far the pleasanter, was at the railroad bridge which spanned a broad creek not far from camp. The duty at this spot was very light, and as the bridge was a covered one, it was in fact the coolest spot anywhere about camp, no small matter in that hot climate. Moreover, the band came there to practice morning and afternoon, having with commendable wisdom selected this cool, shady place for that purpose. The days grew hotter and hotter, and the drills proportionately shorter, and we all began to look forward with wistful longing to the day which should see us safely embarked for home.

CHAPTER XIII.

HOMEWARD BOUND.

THERE had been stories about camp for a day or more, of fighting at Batchelder's Creek, and the death of Colonel Jones, of the 58th Penn., was reported, but we had treated it as a mere rumor. Our astonishment was great when, just before roll-call Sunday evening, May 24th, the order was given to the different companies to prepare for an immediate departure to Batchelder's Creek. The train stood in front of the camp awaiting us, and in twenty minutes from the time the orders were received by the colonel we were on the cars and off for the front.

When the regiment arrived at the picket-station we found everything quiet, but the death of the colonel was confirmed. Two of our companies were immediately sent out on picket, and the rest of us stretched ourselves on the parade-ground for the rest of the night. It appeared that the 58th Penn., in company with two or three other regiments, under command of Colonel Jones, had made a raid up the railroad, and, at the same earthworks we stormed the month before, surprised and captured nearly two hundred prisoners, besides a piece of artillery, baggage-wagons, etc., the general in command barely escaping.

The rebels, receiving large reinforcements from Kinston, pressed closely upon our retiring column, and its gallant commander was shot by a sharpshooter just before reaching the camp. A fight ensued over his body, which resulted in the repulse of the enemy, and the 58th retired within their entrenchments, the joy over their victory wholly overshadowed by the loss of their colonel. The rebels, hearing doubtless of the arrival of reinforcements, had fallen back in the night, and as all fear of an attack was dissipated, we started for our own camp about noon, taking the body of Colonel Jones on the train to Newbern, there to await transportation to his home in Philadelphia. So ended our last expedition in North Carolina.

The following week we were summoned to escort the body of Colonel Jones to the steamer from the house of Captain Messinger, the provost-marshal, in company with all the high officers in the department, who were proud to do honor to the remains of a brave, Christian soldier. After services at the boat we marched back to camp, very tired and dusty, and fully convinced that escort duty at a funeral was no sinecure. The next day General Foster visited the camp, and praising the regiment for its general satisfactory conduct, strongly urged its re-enlistment in his department. The time for such an appeal was unfortunately chosen, just as the men were becoming very weary of military duty, and anxious to see home once more, and the response at the time was not very hearty. But many did ultimately embrace the offer, finding that the excitement of a soldier's life had unfitted them for anything else.

The departure of the 43d and 44th Mass. naturally served to turn our thoughts northward, and we did little else but discuss the chances of a speedy return, talk of our reception, and lay wagers as to the probable time of sailing, etc. As the weather grew warmer, the climate began to have a marked effect upon the health of the regiment. Drill was shortened, and everything possible done to avert the evil; but one after another sickened, until the regimental hospital was crowded, and numbers were sent every day or two to the hospital at Beaufort, to have the benefit of the fresh sea-breeze.

But in vain. The sun beat hotter and hotter on those little tents, until we lived, as it were, in a fiery furnace. The sickness increased daily, and some poor fellows passed on to their resting-place above, when almost in reach of that earthly home towards which their thoughts and dreams had so long been directed. As one after another fell victims to the terrible fever, we began to fear none would be left to return unless the summons came quickly. After much weary waiting, our hearts were rejoiced by the news of the arrival at Morehead City of the steamers "Spaulding" and "Tillie," prepared to transport us from the land of sickness and sorrow to a more genial clime.

Our joy was somewhat lessened by the rumor that we were ordered to report to General Dix, at Fortress Monroe, and if needed, to join the force then operating in the vicinity of the White House, Va.; but that was as nothing in view of the fact that we were actually homeward bound. The night before our departure the following farewell order from General Foster was read to the regiment:

HEADQUARTERS, DEPARTMENT OF NORTH CAROLINA,
18TH ARMY CORPS,
NEWBERN, June 23, 1863.

SPECIAL ORDER NO. 178.

The Commanding General bids farewell to the officers and soldiers of the 45th M. V. M., with the most sincere regret at losing a regiment which has proved itself so good and deserving in every position which it has been called upon to occupy. In the various marches and fights they have exhibited that order, discipline, experience and courage, which he hoped and expected to find in an organization so worthily descended from the "Ancient and Honorable Corps of Boston Cadets." For those who have fallen in the fight or by disease, the General offers his sincere and heartfelt sympathy to their comrades in arms, and to their bereaved friends at home. To those who have survived the dangers, though sharing them, the general bids God Speed!

By command of
Major-General JOHN G. FOSTER.

JOHN F. ANDERSON,
Major and Sen. A. D. C.

On Wednesday morning, the 24th of June, we broke up our camp, leaving everything standing in expectation of its speedy occupation by some other regiment, and embarking on the cars, were hurried towards Beaufort. There we found the vessels awaiting our arrival at the same wharf at which we had landed nearly eight months before, then a happy company, full of life and health, eager to be at work in our country's cause, but now a forlorn and weary number, sick in body and mind, with scarce energy enough left to realize that the hour for which we had longed and prayed so many weary days had come at last.

Sick and well, we were all after a time embarked, and in twenty-four hours were anchored off Fortress Monroe. On mustering the available strength of the regiment, it was found that out of about eight hundred and sixty men but three hundred and fifty were fit for active service. The colonel went on shore to report the condition of the regiment, and, after some delay, received orders from the War Department to proceed with his command directly to Boston, so on Friday afternoon we were once more headed homewards. Most of us were too miserable to display our joy in noisy mirth, but the spirits of the men brightened visibly as the way grew shorter. Two of our number passed away to their eternal home in that short passage, and others survived the voyage only to die in the arms of loved ones at home.

After a bright, calm passage, the "Spaulding" steamed up Boston harbor early Monday morning, the 29th of June, and was quickly boarded by a party of friends who had been cruising about the harbor the whole of the previous day in anticipation of our arrival. After landing the numerous sick at T wharf, the vessel again hauled out into the stream to await the arrival of the "Tilly," which was but a poor sailor. The latter steamer arrived so late in the afternoon that it was deemed advisable to postpone the reception till the following day. The poor fellows were consequently condemned to pass another night on board of crowded transports in full sight of their own homes.

Tuesday dawned as bright and pleasant as heart could desire, and about nine o'clock the regiment landed, and, escorted by the Cadets and Massachusetts Rifle Club, proceeded *en route* for the State House. After a reception by Governor Andrew, it marched to the parade-ground and had a short battalion drill, then, having had a collation, the men were delivered into the arms of their expectant friends.

After all these ceremonies had been gone through with, the regiment went to the old camp at Readville, and having turned over arms and equipments to the quartermaster, were furloughed till the following Monday, when they were mustered out of the United States service, but neither paid nor discharged.

After enjoying the luxuries of home life for about three weeks, the news of the New York riots came upon us in all their horror and wickedness. Symptoms of uneasiness betraying themselves in our own city, a notice appeared in the papers signed by the colonel, requesting the regiment to assemble at Readville on Wednesday, the 15th of July, to aid in quelling any disturbance that might arise. About two hundred of the men obeyed this order, which, in the scattered state of the regiment, was all that could be hoped for on such an unexpected summons.

It seemed quite like old times, meeting once more in the barracks, and making preparations for an expedition, though the consciousness that this time we were only bound to the city of Boston had a very enlivening effect upon us all. The quartermaster furnished us with arms, ammunition and equipments, and, with our blankets slung in the old fashion, we could very easily have imagined ourselves on the point of starting off on a tramp up country from Newbern.

Having formed in line, the colonel equalized the companies, a rather important matter, as the Nantucket company, Co. H, had but one representative besides the officers, and the Cape Cod company, Co. D, but four or five. We then went through a short drill in street firing; and having loaded our guns with ball cartridges, started for the cars and were deposited at the depot in town. Having executed the order, "prime," with guns capped and at half-cock, to show the bystanders and all interested that this did not mean blank cartridges or holiday parade, we marched to our quarters in Faneuil Hall.

This was the day following that of the Cooper street riot, and as a renewed attack on Dock Square and its gun-shops was expected that night, this, the post of danger and honor, was assigned to the 45th, as well as the support of four guns of the 11th Battery, Capt. Jones. We were on duty through the night, half of the regiment at a time, under command of the lieutenant-colonel and major, a company being assigned to each gun, they being placed one at each corner of Faneuil Hall, thus commanding all the streets converging upon Dock Square. There were pickets out on all the neighboring streets, and no persons, except market men, were permitted to enter the square.

Strict orders were given to fire immediately on the approach of any threatening body of people, and thus, by a wise severity at the outset, to prevent such a prolongation of outrages as had resulted from the misjudged leniency of the New York authorities. The night was passed very quietly, excepting some disturbance from a noisy crowd in the evening, which was, however, quickly dispersed by a patrol of dragoons. A regular guard was stationed at the entrance of the building, and there we had to stay throughout the day, short furloughs of an hour or two being occasionally granted There is reason to fear, however, that during the week spent in the hall a good many private furloughs were taken by way of the windows and spouts, but as we were only on duty at night, it mattered but little.

We continued to spend our nights in the open air, generally in the Square, and on one or two occasions detachments were sent to other points, South Boston bridge, the armories, etc. Though the city seemed to be restored to its pristine security, yet fearing some outbreak on Saturday night or Sunday, we were detained till the next Tuesday. It seemed very strange to post sentries about the streets and alleys, with orders to allow no one to pass through, and the indignation of some of our worthy citizens at being made to go some other way, was very amusing .Our days were spent in watching the passers-by from the windows, and one or two afternoons we were treated to a battalion drill on the Common, in which we certainly showed rather how much we had forgotten than what we knew, for our mistakes were very numerous. The gaping crowd were, however, none the wiser, and doubtless thought them all a part of the show.

But all good things must sometime have an end, and so did our rations of bologna sausage and Washington pie, daily served out to us in the Cradle of Liberty. The rioters thought better of their plans, and wisely concluded that it was preferable to run the risk of being drafted and then killed, than to be shot down at their very doors; a fate they had every reason to expect if they attempted any further disturbance of the peace. Thanks to the prompt action of the state and city authorities, the riotous proceedings were nipped in the bud, and law and order again reigned supreme.

The men had been dropping in to the rendezvous from day to day, drawn from a distance by the summons, until we numbered five hundred strong, and on Monday night, knowing it would be the last time we should be together as a regiment, we devoted the evening, for we had no duty to perform that night, to having a good time. We sang all the army songs till we were tired out; cheered all the officers and everything connected with the regiment, individually and collectively, till we were hoarse, and made such a scene as even old Faneuil Hall, in all her long history of stirring events, had never witnessed the like of before, and probably never will again.

Our task was ended, our nine months more than full. Leaving behind us a name blotted by no stain of dishonor, and with a proud consciousness of having done honor to the noble State that gave us birth, having, in camp and on the battle-field, striven to do our duty by the government we had volunteered to serve, on Tuesday, the twenty-first day of July, eighteen hundred and sixty-three, we were paid off and discharged, and the old Forty-Fifth lived only in history.

We had seen every variety of service, life in barracks, in tents and in houses. Our losses in battle, twenty killed and seventy-one wounded, outnumbered that of all the other nine-month's regiments in the department taken together, while our loss from disease was very heavy. Our officers were worthy of their commands, and the men worthy of their commanders. Never, from the commencement of the war, was an officer sent from the State better fitted for the responsibilities of his position than our noble colonel, Charles R. Codman. Perfect in his drill, firm in his discipline, yet free from all severity; brave in the hour of danger, yet without rashness; loved, and yet respected, he was truly a model officer. In the coming years it will be the pride and boast of every member of the 45th Mass. that he served for such a country, in such a cause, from such a State, under such a commander, in such a regiment.

www.ingramcontent.com/pod-product-compliance
Lightning Source LLC
Chambersburg PA
CBHW030247170426
43202CB00009B/656